映画化された英米文学 24
そのさわりを読む

行方　昭夫
河島　弘美
　　　編著

TSURUMI SHOTEN

Credits:

RAIN by William Somerset Maugham
Copyright©1921 by William Somerset Maugham
English language reprint rights arranged with
United Agents Limited, London
through Tuttle-Mori Agency, Inc., Tokyo

A PASSAGE TO INDIA by E. M. Forster
Copyright©1924 by E. M. Forster
English language reprint rights arranged with
The Society of Authors, London
through Tuttle-Mori Agency, Inc., Tokyo

A FAREWELL TO ARMS by Ernest Hemingway
Copyright© 1929 by Ernest Hemingway
Used by permission of Hemingway Foreign Rights Trust
through Japan UNI Agency, Inc., Tokyo

THE GRAPES OF WRATH by John Steinbeck
Copyright© 1939 by John Steinbeck, renewed 1967 by
John Steinbeck
Used by permission of McIntosh and Otis, Inc.
through Japan UNI Agency, Inc., Tokyo

はしがき

　『映画化された英米文学 24　そのさわりを読む』は、欲張った本です。映画、英米文学の名作、英米文学史、名作アンソロジー、英文解釈、英文法、翻訳のいずれかに関心のある人なら、誰にでも役立つように配慮してあります。映画化されている英米文学の代表作から、英米それぞれ 1 ダースを厳選し、各作品について、作家作品の紹介、「さわり」の原文、それを読むための丁寧な注釈、さらに英文法ガイドを巻末に用意しました。

　作家作品の紹介では、作家と作品の特色とあらすじ、及び映画の解説など、多くの情報を圧縮して簡潔に述べました。

　一作につき 500 語ほどの「さわり」は、原作の英語の見本となる有名な箇所の中から、読んで面白く、かつ語彙や構文の面から比較的平易なものを選びました。注釈には、単語や熟語の意味のほか、一般に英語を読むときにも応用がきくように、仮定法や話法など英文法の説明をしました。それだけでなく、必要に応じて文章の隠された意味合いにも言及しています。巻末の英文法ガイドでは、基礎的な知識だけでなく、コンテクスト、描出話法など、中級以上の英文理解に不可欠の解説も加えてあります。注釈の中で、［英文法ガイド 6–V–2］参照、という形で注意を喚起し、具体的な用例によって理解が深まるようにしました。

　本書の題名になっている、文学作品の映画化について、皆さんはどう思われますか？　映画を見て気に入って原作を読む、という場合もあれば、好きな作品が映画化されたので見に行く、という場合もありますね。以前は英米文学の映画化の情報が入ると、翻訳の出版社は多くの読者を見込んで本を大増刷したものでした。今は書物を読む人が少なくなりましたが、それでも大作映画が公開されれば、書店には原作の翻訳が並びます。

　愛読書が原作となっている映画を見た場合、どうしても満足できない人が多いようです。愛読書であればあるほど、登場人物について自分なりのイメージがあるため、俳優がそれに及ばないことが多いのです。自分が一番好きな場面が無いことさえあります。読むのに数日以上かかる原作に対

して、映画は2時間前後で鑑賞できるように作られますから、それも仕方ないのです。でも時には、僅か2時間で原作のエッセンスを見事な映像で見せてくれる映画に出会って感激することもあります。

　映画化には、原作に忠実なものと、原作をヒントにするだけで原作との関係が希薄なものとがあります。原作の舞台は昔なのに、映画では背景が20世紀という場合もあります。本書で取り上げた原作は有名なものばかりなので、映画化される機会が多く、複数の映画の中から自分の好みのものを選ぶことが可能です。いずれの場合も、映画と文学はジャンルが違うのですから、原作との違いにあまり神経質にならず、できるだけ長所を見つける寛大さも大切ではないでしょうか。なお、原作に忠実であることを尊重する人には、BBC制作の連続テレビドラマが好まれるでしょう。

　英文をじっくりと読むことは、以前より軽視されていますが、日本人の英語学習の中心であるべきだと私どもは考えています。表面だけを撫でているような読み方では、退屈なのは確かです。本書の注釈を利用して英文を丁寧に読み、作者の意味するところを正確に理解すれば、英文読解の本当の面白さが実感できます。

　英語は日本語から遠く離れた言語です。英文法を知らずに、英語は理解できません。「さわり」の英文の理解に英文法がいかに有用であるか、多くの実例に接して実感して下さい。

　イギリス文学は行方が、アメリカ文学は河島が担当しましたが、『ジェイン・エア』と『嵐が丘』は河島が、『アッシャー家の崩壊』と『緋文字』は行方が担当しました。両者でそれぞれの原稿を交換してチェックしあい、注釈の正確さに慎重を期しました。

　なお引用の原文は主にペンギン版を使用し、各引用文の末尾に章と頁を記してあります。ペンギン版以外のものの場合には、その旨記してあります。

　本書がたくさんの方々に様々な目的で愛用されるよう念じてやみません。

　2015年10月

行方　昭夫　河島　弘美

CONTENTS

はしがき

イギリス文学編

1. **Romeo and Juliet** by William Shakespeare 3
   『ロミオとジュリエット』ウィリアム・シェイクスピア

2. **Gulliver's Travels** by Jonathan Swift 8
   『ガリバー旅行記』ジョナサン・スウィフト

3. **Pride and Prejudice** by Jane Austen 13
   『高慢と偏見』ジェイン・オースティン

4. **Jane Eyre** by Charlotte Brontë 18
   『ジェイン・エア』シャーロット・ブロンテ

5. **Wuthering Heights** by Emily Brontë 23
   『嵐が丘』エミリー・ブロンテ

6. **Great Expectations** by Charles Dickens 28
   『大いなる遺産』チャールズ・ディケンズ

7. **Tess of the d'Urbervilles** by Thomas Hardy 32
   『ダーバーヴィル家のテス』トマス・ハーディー

8. **"A Scandal in Bohemia"** by Conan Doyle 37
   from The Adventures of Sherlock Holmes
   「ボヘミアの醜聞」(『シャーロック・ホームズの冒険』より) コナン・ドイル

9. **Pygmalion** by George Bernard Shaw 42
   『ピグマリオン (マイ・フェア・レディ)』ジョージ・バーナード・ショー

10. **Rain** by William Somerset Maugham 46
    『雨』サマセット・モーム

11. **A Passage to India** by E. M. Forster 51
    『インドへの道』E. M. フォースター

12. **Lady Chatterley's Lover** by D. H. Lawrence 56
    『チャタレイ夫人の恋人』D. H. ロレンス

アメリカ文学編

1. **The Last of the Mohicans** by James Fenimore Cooper 63
   『モヒカン族の最後』ジェイムズ・フェニモア・クーパー

2. **The Fall of the House of Usher** by Edgar Allan Poe 68
   『アッシャー家の崩壊』エドガー・アラン・ポオ

3. **The Scarlet Letter** by Nathaniel Hawthorne 73
   『緋文字』ナサニエル・ホーソン

4. **Moby Dick: or The Whale** by Herman Melville 78
   『白鯨』ハーマン・メルヴィル

5. **Little Women** by Louisa May Alcott 82
   『若草物語』ルイザ・メイ・オルコット

6. **Washington Square** by Henry James 86
   『ワシントン・スクエア（女相続人）』ヘンリー・ジェイムズ

7. **Adventures of Huckleberry Finn** by Mark Twain 90
   『ハックルベリー・フィンの冒険』マーク・トウェイン

8. **Sister Carrie** by Theodore Dreiser 95
   『シスター・キャリー（黄昏）』セオドア・ドライサー

9. **The Great Gatsby** by F. Scott Fitzgerald 100
   『グレート・ギャツビー』F. スコット・フィッツジェラルド

10. **A Farewell to Arms** by Ernest Hemingway 104
    『武器よさらば』アーネスト・ヘミングウェイ

11. **Gone with the Wind** by Margaret Mitchell 109
    『風と共に去りぬ』マーガレット・ミッチェル

12. **The Grapes of Wrath** by John Steinbeck 113
    『怒りの葡萄』ジョン・スタインベック

英文法ガイド 117

Part 1

イギリス文学編

1.『ロミオとジュリエット』

Romeo and Juliet
(1595?)
by
William Shakespeare

　ウィリアム・シェイクスピア William Shakespeare (1564–1616)。世界中でもっとも広く知られた劇作家です。裕福だった父は、ウィリアムの少年時代に失脚し、彼は小学校より上の学校教育を受けていません。18歳の時、8歳上の女性と結婚、6か月後に長女が、さらに翌々年には双子が生まれました。まもなく単身で上京し劇団に入り、作家として修業したようです。28歳の時に評判の新進劇作家としてロンドンの劇場に登場しました。次第に、独自の境地に達し、20年ほどの間に37の劇を世に送ります。1611年ごろ故郷に引き上げ数年後死亡。創作活動は、一期 (1590–95) の習作時代には史劇『リチャード三世』、喜劇『恋の骨折り損』、悲劇『ロミオトジュリエット』他があります。二期 (1596–1600) は、円熟した喜劇の多い時代で、『夏の夜の夢』、『ヴェニスの商人』、『十二夜』などの喜劇、『ヘンリー四世』などの史劇、『ジュリアス・シーザー』などの悲劇他があります。三期 (1601–09) の悲劇時代は『ハムレット』、『オセロー』、『マクベス』、『リア王』他です。四期 (1610–12) はロマンス劇時代で『テンペスト』他です。

　モンタギュー家のロメオは反目するキャプレット家の舞踏会でジュリエットと出会い、双方強い愛情を覚えます。乳母と修道僧の計らいで結婚。ところがロメオはジュリエットの従兄と喧嘩して殺害し、追放を命じられます。最初で最後の夜を過ごした後、夫は去り、青年貴族との結婚を迫られた妻は、修道僧の指示で、仮死をもたらす秘薬を婚礼の前夜に飲みます。事情を知らせる手紙がロメオに届かず、妻の死を聞いて、墓所に急行、妻の横で服毒自殺します。目を覚ました妻も夫の後を追います。大公は、この悲劇を契機に和解を命じ両家長も応じます。若い恋の美しさを抒情性豊かに歌い上げる感動的な悲劇です。

　オリヴィア・ハッセーが演じるジュリエットは、甘美な音楽もあって、多くの映画観客を魅了しました。

William Shakespeare

(1) 彼がモンタギュー家の長男と知り、ジュリエットはバルコニーで虚空に向かって嘆きます。

JULIET　O Romeo, Romeo! wherefore art thou Romeo?
　Deny thy father and refuse thy name;
　Or, if thou wilt not, be but sworn my love,
　And I'll no longer be a Capulet.
ROMEO [Aside] Shall I hear more, or shall I speak at this?　　　5
JULIET　'Tis but thy name that is my enemy;
　Thou art thyself, though not a Montague.
　What's Montague? it is nor hand, nor foot,
　Nor arm, nor face, nor any other part
　Belonging to a man. O, be some other name!　　　10

Notes •••••

1　**Wherefore art thou** = Why are you.
2　**Deny thy father**　thy = your.　父との縁を絶つというのはモンタギュー家から出るということです。
3　**If thou wilt not, be but sworn my love**「あなたがそうしたくないなら、私への愛を誓いなさい」
　be but sworn my love = be only my sworn love.「ただ私への愛を誓った人になりなさい」が直訳。
4　**And I'll no longer be a Capulet**「そうすれば、私はもうキャピュレット家の一員をやめます」
5　**aside**　傍白。演劇で、観客には聞こえるが相手役には聞こえない想定となっているせりふ。
6　**'Tis but thy name that is my enemy**「私の敵なのはあなたの名前のみ」
7　**Thou art thyself**「あなたはあなた自身よ」

What's in a name? that which we call a rose
By any other name would smell as sweet;
So Romeo would, were he not Romeo call'd,
Retain that dear perfection which he owes
Without that title. Romeo, doff thy name,   15
And for that name which is no part of thee
Take all myself.
ROMEO   I take thee at thy word:
Call me but love, and I'll be new baptized;
Henceforth I never will be Romeo. (II–2)   20

Notes •••••

12 **By any other name would smell as sweet**「他の名前で呼んだとしても、同じくいい香りがするでしょう」仮定法。[英文法ガイド 9–IV–3] 参照。
13 **were he not Romeo call'd**「彼がロミオと呼ばれなくても」上と同じ仮定法。
14 **Retain that dear perfection**「あの貴重な完璧さを保つでしょう」would に続きます。
15 **that title** ロミオという名前の肩書。
    doff「捨てる」
16– **For that name ... Take all myself**「名前の代わりに私の全てを受けいれて」
18 **I take thee at thy word**「おっしゃるようにあなたを受けいれます」
19 **Call me but love, and I'll be new baptized**「愛人と呼んでくえさえすれば、新しい名前を授かったことになる」
    new = newly.
20 **Henceforth I never will be Romeo**「今後は僕はもうロミオではありません」

William Shakespeare

(2) 最初で最後の夫婦としての夜をすごした後朝(きぬぎぬ)の別れの場面です。

JULIET　Wilt thou be gone? it is not yet near day:
　It was the nightingale, and not the lark,
　That pierced the fearful hollow of thine ear;
　Nightly she sings on yon pomegranate-tree:
　Believe me, love, it was the nightingale. 5
ROMEO　It was the lark, the herald of the morn,
　No nightingale: look, love, what envious streaks
　Do lace the severing clouds in yonder east:
　Night's candles are burnt out, and jocund day
　Stands tiptoe on the misty mountain tops. 10
　I must be gone and live, or stay and die.　(III-5)

Notes •••••
1　**Wilt thou be gone?**「行ってしまうの」
　　it is not yet near day「まだ朝ではないわ」
3　**That pierced the fearful hollow of thine ear**「あなたの耳の怯えた穴を貫いたのは…」it…that の強調文です。
6　**The herald of the morn**「朝の使者」
7–　**what envious streaks ... east**「どのような意地悪な光の筋が、あちらの東で、切れ切れの雲を縁取っているか、愛する人よ、見てごらん」が直訳。
9　**Night's candles are burnt out**「夜の燈火が燃え尽きた」
　　jocund day Stands ... tops「楽しい日が霧のかかった山頂に爪先立っている」
11　**I must ... die**「立ち去って生きるか、留まって死ぬかだ」

(3) 最後の両家の和解の場です。

MONTAGUE　But I can give thee more:
　For I will raise her statue in pure gold;
　That while Verona by that name is known,
　There shall no figure at such rate be set
　As that of true and faithful Juliet.　　　　　　　　　　　　　　5
CAPULET　As rich shall Romeo's by his lady's lie;
　Poor sacrifices of our enmity!
PRINCE　A glooming peace this morning with it brings;
　The sun, for sorrow, will not show his head:
　Go hence, to have more talk of these sad things;　　　　　　10
　Some shall be pardon'd, and some punished:
　For never was a story of more woe
　Than this of Juliet and her Romeo. (V–3)

Notes ●●●●

2　**raise her statue in pure gold**「純金のジュリエット像を建造します」
3　**That**「純金なのは以下の目的があってのことです」現在なら so that です。
　while Verona ... known　町の歴史が続く限り、ということ。
4–　**at such rate be set**　このような高級な程度で建てるのは、というのです。
　There shall no figure ... Juliet「誠実で貞節なジュリエット像よりも立派な像は建たないでしょう」語り手の意志を示す shall です。
6　**As rich ... lie**「それに負けぬ立派なロミオ像がその妻のそばに建つ」ここも語り手の意志を示す shall です。
7　**Poor sacrifices of our enmity**「両家の争いの気の毒な犠牲だ」
8　**A glooming ...**　主語は morning で、brings の目的語が peace です。
11　**Some shall ... punished**「許される者もあろうし、罰される者もあろうぞ」権力者の命令口調の一種です。
12–　**For never ... Romeo**「なぜならば、ジュリエットとそのロミオの物語より悲しい物語は存在しなかったからだ」

2. 『ガリヴァー旅行記』

Gulliver's Travels
(1726)
by
Jonathan Swift

　ジョナサン・スウィフト Jonathan Swift (1667–1745) はイギリスの風刺作家。ダブリンで生まれた時に既に父はなく、伯父の援助でダブリン大学を出、先にイングランドに戻っていた母の世話で政治家テンプルの秘書となり、頻繁にアイルランドとイングランドを往復し、イングランド対アイルランド、トーリー党対ウィッグ党など、いずれかを擁護し攻撃する時事的なパンフレットなど鋭い文章を多く書きました。政治家を志したこともありましたが、テンプルの死後、アイルランドに戻り、聖パトリック教会の副司祭（1713年に首席司祭）を務めます。アイルランドの自由のための論考他も迫力ありますが、名を不朽ならしめたのは、『ガリヴァー旅行記』です。精神錯乱して死亡。

　4部の1部は小人国。リリパット国の住民は身長が6フィートほどしかなく、ガリヴァーには、些細な事に大袈裟に対応する人々が愚かしく見えます。隣国との海戦で大活躍したのですが、宮廷の火事を放尿で消火したことで、不敬罪に問われ隣国へ逃亡。2部大人国。ブロブディンナグ国の住民は身長60フィートの巨人。ガリヴァーは農夫に捕まり、見世物として苛められますが、宮廷人に救われます。宮廷の美しい女官に可愛がられて手の平に載せられると、肌のシミやイボが大きく見えて、幻滅。3部空飛ぶ島他。浮かぶ島ラピュタでは、人々は無我夢中で考えごとばかりしています。地上の学士院では、糞尿から食べ物を作る実験に余念がない学者がいます。4部馬の国。理性で生きるフウイヌム（馬）がヤフーと呼ばれる醜悪な動物を支配しています。ヤフーは、貪欲で好色で好戦的で自己中で、ガリヴァーは人間だと気付きますが、馬たちは、彼が理性的なので、ヤフーだと思いません。裸のところを見られてしまい追放されます。帰国し妻と再会、抱きつかれると、悪臭がたまらず気絶します。

　2010年の映画版は、1部と2部のみであり、また時代を現代に移した作品です。他に宮崎作品の「天空の城ラピュタ」などのアニメもあります。

Gulliver's Travels

(1) 小人国でガリヴァーが地面に縛り付けられた場面の画像を見た人は多いでしょうね。

 I attempted to rise, but was not able to stir: for, as I happened to lie on my back, I found my arms and legs were strongly fastened on each side to the ground; and my hair, which was long and thick, tied down in the same manner. I likewise felt several slender ligatures across my body, from my armpits to my thighs. I could only look upwards; the sun began to grow hot, and the light offended my eyes. I heard a confused noise about me, but in the posture I lay, could see nothing except the sky. In a little time I felt something alive moving on my left leg, which advancing gently forward over my breast, came almost up to my chin; when bending my eyes downwards as much as I could, I perceived it to be a human creature not six inches high, with a bow and arrow in his hands, and a quiver at his back. (Pt. I, Ch. 1, pp. 55–56)

Notes ●●●●●

 5 **ligatures**「ひも」
 7– **in the posture I lay**「私が横たわっている姿勢では」
 9– **advancing gently forward over my breast**「胸の上で緩やかに前進して」
 11 **human creature**「人間らしい生き物」
 13 **quiver**「矢筒」

Jonathan Swift

(2) 大人国での体験です。美女がどう見えるのでしょう？

 That which gave me most uneasiness among these Maids of Honour, when my nurse carried me to visit them, was to see them use me without any manner of ceremony, like a creature who had no sort of consequence. For, they would strip themselves to the skin, and put on their smocks in my presence, while I was placed on their toilet directly before their naked bodies, which, I am sure, to me was very far from being a tempting sight, or from giving me any other emotions than those of horror and disgust. Their skins appeared so coarse and uneven, so variously coloured, when I saw them near, with a mole here and there as broad as a trencher, and hairs hanging from it thicker than pack-threads; to say nothing further concerning the rest of their persons. Neither did they at all scruple while I was by to discharge what they had drank, to the quantity of at least two hogsheads, in a vessel that held above three tuns.　(Pt. II, Ch. 5, p. 158)

*N*otes ●●●●●

1　**That which** = what.
1–　**Maids of Honour**　宮廷で働く「女官」
3　**use me without any manner of ceremony**「私をまったく礼儀作法なしで扱う」この use は「扱う」の意味です。
4　**no sort of consequence**「まったく重要でない」
6　**toilet**「化粧台」古い用法。
7　**far from being a tempting sight**「魅力的な光景であることからほど遠い」
9　**coarse and uneven**「ざらざらし、でこぼこしていた」
　　variously coloured「まだらな色がついている」
10–　**as broad as a trencher**「大きな木皿くらいある」
11　**pack-threads**「荷造りひも」
11–　**to say nothing ... of their persons**「身体の他の部分については言うに及ばず」
13　**scruple**「ためらう」主に否定形で使います。not scruple to「ためらわない、平気でする」／ **while I was by**「私が側にいる時」／ **discharge**「排泄する」
14　**hogsheads**　液体の単位で、52.5 ガロン。大樽1つ分。
15　**tuns**　液体の単位で、252 ガロン。

Gulliver's Travels

(3) 浮島ラピュタから地上に降りて訪ねた学士院の研究所でのこと。

I went into another chamber, but was ready to hasten back, being almost overcome with a horrible stink. . . . His employment from his first coming into the Academy, was an operation to reduce human excrement to its original food, by separating the several parts, removing the tincture which it receives from the gall, making the odour exhale, and scumming off the saliva. He had a weekly allowance, from the Society of a vessel filled with human ordure, about the bigness of a Bristol barrel. (Pt. III, Ch. 5, p. 224)

Notes ●●●●●

2 **His employment**「彼の仕事」この意味は古風です。
4 **human excrement**「人の糞便」
4– **separating the several parts**「さまざまな組成物を分離する」
5 **removing the tincture ... gall**「胆汁から生じる色を除去する」
5– **making the odour exhale**「臭気を発散させる」
6 **scumming off the saliva**「沸騰させ浮き滓を取り去る」
7 **human ordure**「人糞」
8 **Bristol barrel**「ブリストルのワインの大樽」

Jonathan Swift

(4) 少なくとも「馬の国」は児童文学とはとうてい言えませんね。

 The master horse ordered a sorrel nag, one of his servants, to untie the largest of these animals, and take him into the yard. The beast and I were brought close together, and by our countenances diligently compared, both by master and servant, who thereupon repeated several times the word *Yahoo*. My horror and astonishment are not to be described, when I observed, in this abominable animal, a perfect human figure. (Pt. IV, Ch. 2, p. 276)

*N*otes ●●●●●
1 **sorrel nag**「栗毛の小馬」
3 **by our countenances**「ヤフーと私の顔のよって（較べられた）」
4 **thereupon**「比較した結果として」
6 **are not to be described**「描くのは不可能だ」［英文法ガイド 3-I-4］参照。

3.『高慢と偏見』

Pride and Prejudice
(1813)
by
Jane Austen

　ジェイン・オースティン Jane Austen (1775–1817) は 18 世紀と 19 世紀の境目の時期に、イギリス小説の本道の作品を書いた女流作家。イングランドで生まれました。父は牧師で、ジェインには 6 名の兄弟と 1 名の姉がいまして、彼女は牧師館で 25 年暮らしました。父引退後は、バースに 5 年、サウサンプトンに 3 年、没するまでの年月は故郷のチョートンで暮らしました。上流中産階級で貧しくはないけれど、裕福でもなく、女性は家庭で教育を受け、英文学、フランス語を身に付けました。家で家事、針仕事、読書、音楽、社交、舞踏会、ロンドンへの旅などをしました。生涯独身でしたが、好きな男性がいたけれど、急死したと伝えられています。年若い頃から、村の家族についての小説を書いていました。創作活動は前期 (1796–1803)、後期 (1811–16) があり、『分別と多感』『ノーサンガー寺院』『高慢と偏見』が前期、『マンスフィールド・パーク』『エマ』『説得』が後期です。彼女は「小説の題材は田舎の 3、4 家族が丁度いい」と言ったそうですが、守備範囲を守り、村の日常、恋愛、結婚を機智とユーモアと多少の皮肉で活写しました。前期では人の愚行を明るく笑い飛ばしていたのですが、後期ではやや皮肉が強まってきた印象を与えます。

　この小説では、ベネット家の 5 人娘の結婚相手を見つけるのが夫人の最大の関心事です。近所の邸に裕福な青年ビングリが引越してきます。青年は長女と仲良くなります。邸の舞踏会にビングリの友人ダーシーも参加、次女エリザベスはダーシーが高慢だと感じて彼に偏見を抱きます。エリザベスは彼に求婚されても、最初は断るのですが、彼のよい噂や善行を知り、最後にはダーシーを愛するようになります。高慢だというのは、自分の偏見だったと覚るわけで、一篇はエリザベスの成長をたどる明るい小説になっています。映像化はナイトレ主演の映画でもよいですが、BBC 制作で NHK でも放送した連続ドラマがお勧めです。

Jane Austen

冒頭から続けて読みます。ベネット家の夫妻は娘たちの結婚について、共に気にしているものの、表面上の会話では温度差が大きいです。

It is a truth universally acknowledged, that a single man in possession of a good fortune, must be in want of a wife.

However little known the feelings or views of such a man may be on his first entering a neighbourhood, this truth is so well fixed in the minds of the surrounding families, that he is considered the rightful property of some one or other of their daughters. →

*N*otes ●●●●●
1 **It is a truth universally acknowledged ...** とても有名な一節です。It は that 以下を指します。「世界中で認められた真実」というと随分大袈裟ですね。万有引力の法則というようなものだと言うのでしょうか？「財産を持つ独身男なら妻を欲しているに決まっている」それが真理ですか？ 軽く揶揄するような筆致であるのに気付きましょう。
3 **However little known ...** ここは強調のために語順が通常ではありません。主語は the feelings or views of such a man です。全体で「このような男性の感情なり見解なりがどれほど僅かしか知られていなくても」となります。
4 **on his first entering** 「初めて入って来た時に」[英文法ガイド 6-5-1] 参照。
4– **so well fixed ... that** 構文が so ... that であるのを直ぐに気付いて下さい。

Pride and Prejudice

→ "My dear Mr. Bennet," said his lady to him one day, "have you heard that Netherfield Park is let at last?"

Mr. Bennet replied that he had not.

"But it is," returned she; "for Mrs. Long has just been here, and she told me all about it."

Mr. Bennet made no answer.

"Do not you want to know who has taken it?" cried his wife impatiently.

"*You* want to tell me, and I have no objection to hearing it."

This was invitation enough.

"Why, my dear, you must know, Mrs. Long says that Netherfield is taken by a young man of large fortune from the north of England; that he came down on Monday in a chaise and four to see the place, and was so much delighted with it, that he agreed with Mr. Morris immediately; that he is to take possession before Michaelmas, and some of his servants are to be in the house by the end of next week." →

Notes ●●●●●

- 7 **My dear Mr. Bennet** この呼びかけは、苛立ちが込められている場合が多いのですよ。妻は一生懸命なのに、夫が無関心で非協力的なので、やや不満なのです。
- 8 **Netherfield Park is let** 「ネザーフィールド邸が借りられる」大きな邸は固有の名でよばれることが多い。Cf. Mansfield Park（オースチンの小説の題名）
- 10 **But it is** 後に let が省略されていますね。
- 16 **invitation enough** 十分なお喋りへの誘いです。
- 19 **a chaise and four** 3人乗り4頭立て4輪馬車。
- 21 **Michaelmas** 「聖ミカエル祭」9月29日の祭日。

Jane Austen

→ "What is his name?"

"Bingley."

"Is he married or single?"

"Oh! Single, my dear, to be sure! A single man of large fortune; four or five thousand a year. What a fine thing for our girls!"

"How so? How can it affect them?"

"My dear Mr. Bennet," replied his wife, "how can you be so tiresome! You must know that I am thinking of his marrying one of them."

"Is that his design in settling here?"

"Design! nonsense, how can you talk so! But it is very likely that he *may* fall in love with one of them, and therefore you must visit him as soon as he comes."

"I see no occasion for that. You and the girls may go, or you may send them by themselves, which perhaps will be still better, for as you are as handsome as any of them, Mr. Bingley might like you the best of the party." →

Notes ●●●●

- 27 **Oh! Single, my dear, to be sure!** ここにも苛立ちが出ています。「聞くまでもないでしょ！」というのです。
- 28 **four or five thousand a year**「年収が4乃至5千ポンド」不動産収入です。
- 29 **How can it affect them?**「そのことが家の娘たちにどう影響するのかね」夫は面白がって妻をからかっている様子。
- 30 **My dear Mr. Bennet**「何を言っているのよ、いい加減にして」という感じ。
- 31 **tiresome**「苛々させる」
- 31– **marrying one of them**「誰か一人を（その男性と）結婚させる」
- 33 **his design**「意図」この語には「陰謀」という意味があり、今の場合には大袈裟なので、妻が夫の発言をたしなめているのです。
- 37 **I see no occasion for that**「私が訪問する理由が見えない」
- 38 **send them by themselves**「娘たちだけで訪問させる」
- 40 **the party**「一行」

Pride and Prejudice

→ "My dear, you flatter me. I certainly *have* had my share of beauty, but I do not pretend to be anything extraordinary now. When a woman has five grown-up daughters, she ought to give over thinking of her own beauty."

"In such cases, a woman has not often much beauty to think of." 45

"But, my dear, you must indeed go and see Mr. Bingley when he comes into the neighbourhood."

"It is more than I engage for, I assure you."

"But consider your daughters. Only think what an establishment it would be for one of them. Sir William and Lady Lucas are 50 determined to go, merely on that account, for in general, you know, they visit no newcomers. Indeed you must go, for it will be impossible for *us* to visit him, if you do not." (Ch. 1, pp. 5–6)

*N*otes ●●●●●

41　**you flatter me**「褒められて嬉しいわ」という感じです。flatter には「こびへつらう」と「よろこばせる」と、相反する2つの意味があり、コンテクストからどちらであるか判断します。［英文法ガイド12］参照。

41–　**my share of beauty**　若い頃はそれなりに美人だった、ということ。文字通りには「美の分け前に私もありついた」です。

42　**anything extraordinary now**「今では特に美しい（わけでない）」

43–　**give over**「やめる」

45　**much beauty to think of**　自分の美について考えるのをやめるべき、というが、そもそも考えるに値する美などあまり所持しないのだろう、と言うのです。

48　**more than ... you**「本当に、私に約束できる以上のこと」

49　**what an establishment**「どんなにすばらしい家になるか」例えば what a day とあれば、「何といういい事だ」か「どんなに悪い事だ」かのいずれです。これもコンテクストで判断します。

50　**it would be**　仮定法です。「もし成功すれば」の話です。

4.『ジェイン・エア』

Jane Eyre
(1847)
by
Charlotte Brontë

　シャーロット・ブロンテ Charlotte Brontë (1816–55) は、イギリス北部ヨークシャー州の牧師の家に生まれました。五歳の年に母が亡くなり、子供たちは伯母の世話を受けてハワースの牧師館で成長します。六人のうち無事に成人したのはシャーロットと弟一人、妹二人の四人で、ブロンテ三姉妹と呼ばれるのはこのシャーロットとエミリー、アンです。

　シャーロットは住み込みの家庭教師をし、またエミリーとともにベルギーに学びました。帰国後に妹たちとの共著として出した『詩集』(1846) にはほとんど反響がなく、次の小説『教授』は出版社に受け取ってもらえませんでした。しかし、「もっと波瀾に富んだ物語を」という返送時のコメントをきっかけに生まれた『ジェイン・エア』成功のおかげで、エミリーの『嵐が丘』、アンの『アグネス・グレイ』も広く世に出ることができたのです。その後シャーロットは『シャーリー』『ヴィレット』などの作品を発表しますが、結婚後わずか半年で亡くなりました。

　『ジェイン・エア』には、「自伝」という副題がついています。寄宿学校での生活、姉二人の早世、弟の堕落などの体験を基に書かれた部分はありますが、それでも決して豊富とはいえない現実の体験から豊かな一編を書き上げたシャーロットの想像力と創作力には驚きます。主人公のジェインは孤児で、惨めな境遇から寄宿学校時代を経て家庭教師となり、屋敷の主人ロチェスターと出会って結婚式にまで至りますが、式当日に驚くべき秘密が判明して結婚は中止、ジェインは屋敷を出ます。そして試練の末に幸せな結婚に至るまでの半生をジェイン自身が語る一人称小説です。長く読み継がれ、映画、演劇、テレビドラマなどでも人気は衰えません。ひたむきなジェインの人柄を反映した語りが原作の魅力の一つで、時代順に進むわかりやすさ、個性的な登場人物などと相まって、読者をひきつけます。一方映画では原作の各場面がどう構成されているか、容貌に恵まれていない点が強調されているジェインとロチェスターをどんな俳優がどう演じるかも見どころです。

Jane Eyre

(1) 自分とともにインドに行くべきだというセント・ジョンの説得に、ジェインは屈しそうになっています。

All the house was still; for I believe all, except St. John and myself, were now retired to rest. The one candle was dying out: the room was full of moonlight. My heart beat fast and thick: I heard its throb. Suddenly it stood still to an inexpressible feeling that thrilled it through, and passed at once to my head and extremities. The feeling was not like an electric shock; but it was quite as sharp, as strange, as startling: it acted on my senses as if their utmost activity hitherto had been but torpor; from which they were now summoned, and forced to wake. They rose expectant: eye and ear waited, while the flesh quivered on my bones.

'What have you heard? What do you see?' asked St. John. I saw nothing: but I heard a voice somewhere cry—

'Jane! Jane! Jane!' nothing more.

'Oh God! what is it?' I gasped. →

Notes ●●●●

1 **St. John**「セント・ジョン」ジェインのいとこで牧師。宣教師としてインドに赴く決意が固く、一緒に連れて行くためジェインを妻にと望んでいます。
2 **retired to rest**「就寝する、床に就く」上品な言い回しです。
3 **My heart beat fast and thick**「私の心臓の鼓動が速く激しくなった」
4– **it stood still to ... extremities**「心臓をすっかりわくわくさせ、すぐに頭と手足にまで及んだ、表現できない感情を覚えて停止した」extremities (文語)「手足」
7– **their utmost activity**　their = of my senses.
8 **but torpor**「無活発にすぎない」
　 from which　which の先行詞は torpor です。they は my senses。

Charlotte Brontë

I might have said, 'Where is it?' for it did not seem in the room—nor in the house—nor in the garden: it did not come out of the air—nor from under the earth—nor from overhead. I had heard it—where, or whence, for ever impossible to know! And it was the voice of a human being—a known, loved, well-remembered voice—that of Edward Fairfax Rochester; and it spoke in pain and woe wildly, eerily, urgently.

'I am coming!' I cried. 'Wait for me! Oh, I will come!' I flew to the door, and looked into the passage: it was dark. I ran out into the garden: it was void.

'Where are you?' I exclaimed.

The hills beyond Marsh Glen sent the answer faintly back—'Where are you?' I listened. The wind sighed low in the firs: all was moorland loneliness and midnight hush. (Ch. 35, pp. 466–67)

Notes ●●●●

15　**might have said**「～と言ってもよかったかもしれない」
20　**Edward Fairfax Rochester**「エドワード・フェアファクス・ロチェスター」家庭教師をしていた時のジェインの雇い主。彼に妻のいることが結婚式当日に判明したため、ジェインは屋敷を出、セント・ジョンに出会ったのです。
21　**eerily**「不気味に」
22　**I am coming**「すぐに参ります」come は「話し手が相手のところに行く、近づく」
26　**Marsh Glen**　marsh は湿地、沼地　glen は峡谷のこと。
28　**moorland**（主に英）「（ヒースの多い）荒野、湿原」

Jane Eyre

(2) ジェインはファーンディーンの領主館にいるというロチェスターを訪ねます。

 This parlour looked gloomy: a neglected handful of fire burnt low in the grate; and, leaning over it, with his head supported against the high, old-fashioned mantelpiece, appeared the blind tenant of the room. His old dog, Pilot, lay on one side, removed out of the way, and coiled up as if afraid of being inadvertently trodden upon. Pilot pricked up his ears when I came in; then he jumped up with a yelp and a whine, and bounded towards me: he almost knocked the tray from my hands. I set it on the table; then patted him, and said softly, 'Lie down!' Mr. Rochester turned mechanically to *see* what the commotion was: but as he *saw* nothing, he returned and sighed. →

Notes ●●●●

1 **parlour**「居間」
3– **the blind tenant of the room**（火事のために今は目が不自由になった）ロチェスターのこと。
4 **Pilot**「パイロット」ロチェスターの愛犬の名前。
4– **removed out of the way**「人の邪魔にならないように」
5 **inadvertently**「うっかりして」
6 **pricked up his ears**「耳をぴんと立てた」犬や馬の動作。ここではパイロットがジェインの出現に気づいたことを示しています。
7 **yelp**「キャン」というような、短く鋭い声。
 whine 犬がクンクンと鼻を鳴らす音。
 bound「跳ねる、弾む」パイロットの喜びが表れた足取りの形容。
10 **mechanically** この語を訳すのに「機械的に」一辺倒は困りもの。この機会にぜひ辞書を確認しましょう。ここでは目が不自由になったロチェスターが犬の興奮の理由を「見よう」として「無意識に」振り返ったのです。see と saw がイタリックになっている点も見逃さないように。

Charlotte Brontë

→ 'Give me the water, Mary,' he said.

I approached him with the now only half-filled glass. Pilot followed me, still excited.

'What is the matter?' he inquired.

'Down, Pilot!' I again said. He checked the water on its way to his lips, and seemed to listen: he drank, and put the glass down. 'This is you, Mary, is it not?'

'Mary is in the kitchen,' I answered.

He put out his hand with a quick gesture, but not seeing where I stood, he did not touch me. 'Who is this? Who is this?' he demanded, trying, as it seemed, to *see* with those sightless eyes—unavailing and distressing attempt! 'Answer me—speak again!' he ordered, imperiously and aloud.

'Will you have a little more water, sir? I spilt half of what was in the glass,' I said.

'*Who* is it? *What* is it? Who speaks?'

'Pilot knows me, and John and Mary know I am here. I came only this evening,' I answered. (Ch. 37, pp. 481–82)

Notes ●●●●

12 **Mary**「メアリ」夫であるジョンとともにロチェスターの世話をしている女性の名前。ロチェスターは水を求めて呼び鈴を鳴らしたので、当然メアリがコップを持って来たものと思って、こう呼びかけています。

16 **Down**（犬への命令）「伏せ」
checked「とどめた」

17 **listen** 注意して聞く様子。パイロットへの命令の声に、いつものメアリとはどこか違うものを感じたに相違ありません。まさかジェインが戻って来たとはにわかに信じられないロチェスターの様子が巧みに描かれている場面です。

5.『嵐が丘』

Wuthering Heights
(1847)
by
Emily Brontë

　エミリー・ブロンテ Emily Brontë (1818–48) は、いわゆるブロンテ三姉妹の中の二番目で、『ジェイン・エア』の作者シャーロットの妹にあたります。三歳の時に母を失い、母代わりの伯母に育てられました。妹のアンと同様におとなしい性格で、生涯のほとんどを家から離れずに過ごしました。残された作品としては二百編近くの詩がありますが、小説としては Ellis Bell の名で 1847 年に発表した『嵐が丘』一作のみです。その後健康が衰え、三十歳の若さで世を去りました。

　『嵐が丘』は、作者の故郷であるイギリス北部ヨークシャー州の荒涼たる自然を背景とする二家族三代にわたる悲劇で、若い女性作家のペンから生まれたとは思えないほど激しい一編です。サマセット・モームの『世界の十大小説』の一冊に選ばれ、世界中で読まれてきた古典であるばかりでなく、映画や舞台でも繰り返し取り上げられてきた名作です。

　物語は、人間嫌いを自称するロックウッドが屋敷を借りた縁で家主のヒースクリフに会う場面から始まります。ロックウッドが、屋敷で長く家政婦を勤めてきたネリー・ディーンから両家にまつわる昔話を聞き、それを読者に語るという二重の構造になっています。

　ここでは小説の冒頭場面と、キャサリンがヒースクリフへの思いを語る有名な部分を読んでみましょう。ヒースクリフは、ヒンドリーとキャサリン兄妹の父親アーンショー氏に拾われて嵐が丘の屋敷に来た孤児の少年です。キャサリンとはとても気が合う一方、兄のヒンドリーには嫌われ、いじめられます。やがてキャサリンが隣家スラッシュクロス屋敷のエドガーの求愛を受け入れたと知って姿を消し、三年後に紳士となって戻って来ると復讐を誓って着々と両家を手中に収めようとするのです。復讐は次の世代に引き継がれ、キャサリンの娘で同名のキャサリン、ヒンドリーの息子ヘアトン、そしてヒースクリフの息子リントンらが登場します。小説はロックウッドが三つの墓を訪れる場面で結ばれますが、映画版はそれぞれのアレンジで作られています。

Emily Brontë

(1) 小説の冒頭、語り手ロックウッドが家主ヒースクリフを訪ねる場面です。

  1801.—I have just returned from a visit to my landlord—the solitary neighbour that I shall be troubled with. This is certainly a beautiful country! In all England, I do not believe that I could have fixed on a situation so completely removed from the stir of society. A perfect misanthropist's Heaven—and Mr Heathcliff and I are 5 such a suitable pair to divide the desolation between us. A capital fellow! He little imagined how my heart warmed towards him when I beheld his black eyes withdraw so suspiciously under their brows, as I rode up, and when his fingers sheltered themselves, with a jealous resolution, still further in his waistcoat, as I announced my 10 name.
 'Mr Heathcliff?' I said.
 A nod was the answer. →

*N*otes •••••

1- **the solitary neighbor ... with**「僕が悩まされるであろう唯一の隣人」が直訳です。
3- **could have fixed ... society**「これほど世間の騒がしさから隔絶した場所を見つけられるだろう」仮定法過去完了。「いくら懸命に探したとしても」という内容の if が隠されています。［英文法ガイド 9–IV–3］参照。
5 **misanthropist**「人間嫌い（の人）」
  Heathcliff「ヒースクリフ」
6 **capital**（英口語）「すばらしい」
7 **warmed towards him**「彼に対して心が和んだ」
9 **rode up**　ride は「馬に乗って行く」、up は「(話し手・ある場所・時に向かって) 近づく、進んで行く」
  his fingers sheltered themselves「彼の指が身を隠した」
10 **jealous**「油断のない、用心深い」

→ 'Mr Lockwood, your new tenant, sir—I do myself the honour of calling as soon as possible after my arrival, to express the hope that I have not inconvenienced you by my perseverance in soliciting the occupation of Thrushcross Grange: I heard, yesterday, you had had some thoughts—'

'Thrushcross Grange is my own, sir,' he interrupted, wincing, 'I should not allow any one to inconvenience me, if I could hinder it—walk in!'

The 'walk in' was uttered with closed teeth and expressed the sentiment, 'Go to the Deuce!' Even the gate over which he leant manifested no sympathising movement to the words; and I think that circumstance determined me to accept the invitation: I felt interested in a man who seemed more exaggeratedly reserved than myself. (Ch. 1, p. 3)

Notes ••••

14–**I do myself the honour of calling**「訪問という形で敬意を表する」
16　**perseverance**「頑張ること、根気強いこと」ロックウッドは何を頑張ったのか、前後から考えてみましょう。あとに続く in ～ にその説明があります。
17　**Thrushcross Grange**「スラッシュクロス屋敷」ここではまだ、ロックウッドにとっても読者にとっても単に屋敷の名前にすぎませんが、物語中で重要な屋敷であることがやがてわかります。
20–　**I should not allow ... hinder it**「私に不都合になるようなことは、それが避けられる限り、誰にもさせておかないだろう」が直訳。
23　**sentiment**「意味」
　　Go to the Deuce「とっとと失せろ」deuce = devil.
24　**manifested no sympathizing ... words**「言葉に同調するような動きはまったく見せなかった」が直訳。中に入るように相手に言いながら、扉に寄りかかったままなのです。
24–　**I think that circumstance ... invitation**「そういう状況が、僕を入って行く気にさせたのだと思う」
25–　**felt interested**「興味をかきたてられた」[英文法ガイド 7-3] 参照。
26　**reserved**「よそよそしい、打ち解けない」

Emily Brontë

(2) キャサリンが台所のネリーのところに来て、エドガーのプロポーズを承諾したと話します。

 'It is not,' retorted she, 'it is the best! The others were the satisfaction of my whims; and for Edgar's sake, too, to satisfy him. This is for the sake of one who comprehends in his person my feelings to Edgar and myself. I cannot express it; but surely you and every body have a notion that there is, or should be, an 5
existence of yours beyond you. What were the use of my creation if I were entirely contained here? My great miseries in this world have been Heathcliff's miseries, and I watched and felt each from the beginning; my great thought in living is himself. →

*N*otes ●●●●

1 **It is not.** この引用部分の直前で、「エドガーと結婚すればヒースクリフを助けられる」というキャサリンの考えについて「今までにあなたが挙げた結婚の理由の中で一番良くない」と述べたネリーに対し、そんなことはないとキャサリンが反論しています。
  the others「他の理由」
2 **and for Edgar's sake** the others はここにもかかります。
  Edgar「エドガー」スラッシュクロスに住むリントン家の長男。キャサリンは結婚の相手としてエドガーを選んだのです。
5– **an existence of yours beyond you**「自分を越えた自分という存在」you は一般人称。
6– **What were the use ... contained here?**「私がここにおさまっているだけですべてだったとしたら、神さまが私をおつくりになったことにどんな意味があるの?」修辞疑問です。
8 **each** 後に misery が省略されています。

Emily Brontë

→ If all else perished, and *he* remained, I should still continue to be; and if all else remained, and he were annihilated, the Universe would turn to a mighty stranger. I should not seem a part of it. My love for Linton is like the foliage in the woods. Time will change it, I'm well aware, as winter changes the trees—my love for Heathcliff resembles the eternal rocks beneath—a source of little visible delight, but necessary. Nelly, I *am* Heathcliff—he's always, always in my mind—not as a pleasure, any more than I am always a pleasure to myself—but, as my own being—so, don't talk of our separation again—it is impracticable; and—'

She paused, and hid her face in the folds of my gown; but I jerked it forcibly away. I was out of patience with her folly!

(Ch. 9, pp. 81–82)

Notes ●●●●

10　**he**　ヒースクリフを指すのはもちろんですが、イタリック体で強調されています。
　　I should still continue to be「私は存在し続けるでしょう」
11-　**turn to a mighty stranger**「ひどくよそよそしいものになる」
13　**Linton**「リントン」エドガーのこと。
15-　**a source of little ... necessary**「目に見える喜びの源にはほとんどならないが、必要なもの」
16　**I am Heathcliff**　イタリック体になっているのは強調のしるし。「私はヒースクリフ」有名なせりふです。
17　**any more than ... to myself**「私が常に私自身の喜びとは限らないのと同様に」
18　**but, as my own being**「私そのものとして」not ... but の表現です。
18-　**our separation** = separation of Heathcliff and myself.
20　**gown**「ドレス」
21　**out of patience**「愛想をつかして、我慢できなくなって」

6.『大いなる遺産』

Great Expectations
(1860–61)
by
Charles Dickens

　チャールズ・ディケンズ Charles Dickens (1812–70) は、イギリスではシェイクピアにつぐ国民的作家です。クリスマスの時期に、スクルージが親切な人に変身する『クリスマス・キャロル』を思い出さない人はいません。ディケンズは、父の負債のため債務者監獄に入れられ、靴墨工場で働くなど、惨めな少年時代を送りました。独学で勉強し、弁護士の書記、速記者、新聞のレポーターなどとして働き、ロンドンでの見聞を軽妙な文章で書くなどして、次第に文才を認められました。雑誌に連載した『ピクウィック・ペイパーズ』が爆発的な人気を呼び、文名が確立。代表作としては『オリヴァ・ツイスト』、『骨董店』、『デイヴィッド・コパフィールド』、『荒涼館』、『二都物語』、『大いなる遺産』など。社会のひずみを笑いと悲哀をまじえて描きました。作中人物は、多くが一面を強調した、その意味では平板な人物でしたが、それだけに読者には分かりやすく、強い印象を残しました。社会問題に関心が深く、『オリヴァ・ツイスト』では、孤児が空腹を訴える場面を鮮明に描き、大きな話題となり、貧民法の改正につながりました。渡米した時には、奴隷廃止を主張したこともありました。

　主人公のピップは、早く両親を亡くし、年長の姉とその親切な夫で鍛冶屋の家で暮らしています。墓地で脱獄犯を助けたり、近所の邸で美少女で意地悪なエステラと知りあったりします。邸のハヴィシャム婦人は、昔結婚式の当日に新郎に捨てられたので、男への復讐を生き甲斐にしています。ある日突然鍛冶屋にロンドンの弁護士が訪問してきて、ピップが莫大な遺産をいずれ受け取ることになったと告げられ、そのためロンドンで紳士になるための教育を受けることになります。上京したピップが、紳士としてどう変貌するのか、エステラとの関係はどう発展するのか、遺産を与えようとした人物が一体誰なのかなどが、徐々に解き明かされます。原作を見事に生かしたリーン監督の古い白黒映画がお勧めです。

Great Expectations

(1) ピップが両親の墓のある教会の墓地に来たとき突然見知らぬ男が現れます。I はピップです。

"Hold your noise!" cried a terrible voice, as a man started up from among the graves at the side of the church porch. "Keep still, you little devil, or I'll cut your throat!"

A fearful man, all in coarse gray, with a great iron on his leg. A man with no hat, and with broken shoes, and with an old rag tied round his head. A man who had been soaked in water, and smothered in mud, and lamed by stones, and cut by flints, and stung by nettles, and torn by briars; who limped, and shivered, and glared, and growled; and whose teeth chattered in his head as he seized me by the chin.

"Oh! Don't cut my throat, sir," I pleaded in terror. "Pray don't do it, sir."

"Tell us your name!" said the man. "Quick!"

"Pip, sir." (Ch. 1, p. 4)

Notes •••••

1　**Hold your noise**　方言です。文字通りには「音を抑えろ」ですから、「静かにしろ」とか「黙れ」などという意味だと想像はつきますね。
　　started up　文脈から考えて、「出発する」は違う意味でしょうね。start up で「急に立ち上る」という意味の熟語。

3　**little devil**「チビの悪魔」ではなくて、「小僧っ子」
　　or　命令形の後にある場合の意味は？

4　**coarse gray**「ごわごわした生地の灰色の服」
　　a great iron「大きな足かせ」

6–　**soaked in water, and smothered in mud, and lamed by stones**「水にぬらされ、泥に覆われ、石でびっこにならされ」が直訳。

7–　**cut by flints, and stung by nettles, and torn by briars**「火打石で切られ、イラクサで刺され、イバラでひっかき傷を作られた」が直訳。これだけ悪い意味の動詞が受身で並ぶと、男が被害者だという印象になりますね。

8–　**glared, and growled**「にらみつけ、うなり声を出した」

9–　**seized me by the chin**「彼の頭をたたく」に相当する英語が strike him on the head であるのと同じ。

13–　**Tell us your name**　me でなく us と言うのは、俗語です。

Charles Dickens

(2) 脱獄囚だった男が紳士になったピップを突然訪ねてきて、お前を紳士にしたのは自分だと打ち明けます。

"Yes, Pip, dear boy, I've made a gentleman on you! It's me wot has done it! I swore that time, sure as ever I earned a guinea, that guinea should go to you. I swore arterwards, sure as ever I spec'lated and got rich, you should get rich. I lived rough, that you should live smooth; I worked hard, that you should be above work. What odds, dear boy? Do I tell it, fur you to feel a obligation? Not a bit. I tell it, fur you to know as that there hunted dunghill dog wot you kep life in, got his head so high that he could make a gentleman—and, Pip, you're him!" (Ch. 39, p. 319)

Notes ●●●●●

1　**made a gentleman on you**「お前を紳士にした」on は普通は of です。
2　**wot** = who, that. 俗語、方言。
　　sure as ever I earned a guinea「俺が1ギニーを稼いだ時には必ず」
3　**artewards** = afterwards.
4　**spec'lated** = speculated.「投資をした」
　　that you should live smooth「お前が安楽に暮らせるように」that = so that.
5　**be above work**「働かなくて済むように」above は「の上にある」という意味合いです。この時代の紳士の定義は「額に汗して働かない人」でした。
6　**What odds**「いかなるいいことがあるかって?」
　　fur you to feel a obligation　fur = for. a = an.「お前に（俺への）恩を感じさせるためか?」
7–　**as that there hunted dunghill dog ... make a gentleman**　俗語などで分かりにくいでしょう。標準的な英語で書き直せば、次のようになります。that that hunted dunghill dog, whom you had given life, got his head so high that he could make a gentleman.「お前が命を与えた、あの追跡されたくそ野良犬が、堂々と生き抜いて、紳士を生み出すことが出来たということ」
8　**wot you kep life in**　無理に書き直せば、in whom you kept life「お前が命を与えたところの」となります。沼地でピップが彼にパンを与えたことへの言及。
　　got his head so high「理想を掲げてとても頑張った」
9　**you're him**「お前が、その紳士なのだ」

Great Expectations

(3) ピップとエステラが結ばれるということを暗示する場面です。

"Glad to part again, Estella? To me, parting is a painful thing. To me, the remembrance of our last parting has been ever mournful and painful."

"But you said to me," returned Estella, very earnestly, "'God bless you, God forgive you!' And if you could say that to me then, you will not hesitate to say that to me now—now, when suffering has been stronger than all other teaching, and has taught me to understand what your heart used to be. I have been bent and broken, but—I hope—into a better shape. Be as considerate and good to me as you were, and tell me we are friends."

"We are friends," said I, rising and bending over her, as she rose from the bench.

"And will continue friends apart," said Estella.

I took her hand in mine, and we went out of the ruined place; and, as the morning mists had risen long ago when I first left the forge, so, the evening mists were rising now, and in all the broad expanse of tranquil light they showed to me, I saw the shadow of no parting from her. (Ch. 59, p. 484)

*N*otes ●●●●

4 **returned**「言葉を返した」
4– **God bless you, God forgive you!** 祈願文。[英文法ガイド 9. IV. 6] 参照。
5– **then ... now**「あの時」と「今」ですね。ここでは、「あの時〜だったのなら今だって」と肯定しています。
8– **bent and broken ... into a better shape**「捻じ曲げられ、壊されたけど、前より良い形になった」が直訳。
13 **And will continue friends apart** 省略された主語は we ですね。「離れていても友人同士です」
15– **when I first left the forge**「最初あの鍛冶屋から出て行った時に」ピップが住んでいた姉夫妻の鍛冶屋を後にしてロンドンに行った昔のことです。
16– **in all the broad expanse of tranquil light**「広々とした静かな月光の中に」
17– **saw the shadow of no parting from her**「彼女が再度別れようと言い出さないという気配を感じた」二人が遂に結ばれるということが暗示されます。

7.『ダーバーヴィル家のテス』

Tess of the d'Urbervilles
(1891)
by
Thomas Hardy

　トマス・ハーディ Thomas Hardy (1840–1928) は、多くの小説と壮大な劇詩で日本でも人気のヴィクトリア朝最大の小説家、詩人。南イングランドのドーセット州の石工の父の関係で、建築家の弟子になりましたが、病気になり、小説や詩を執筆。メレディスに褒められたのが処女作『窮余の策』です。以後もドーセット州の農村社会と農民たちの人生を写実的に描く小説を書いて行きます。世界を支配するのは、人間の苦悩に無関心な盲目的な「内在的な意志」Immanent Will であり、それと戦い翻弄される人間を描くのを自分の使命だとしました。『帰郷』、『カースタブリッジの町長』、『ダーバーヴィル家のテス』、『日陰者ジュード』が長編で、短編も多い。晩年は、小説の筆を折り、叙事詩『覇王たち』を執筆。

　貧しい世間知らずの美しい娘テスが、運命に翻弄される話です。金持ちの家の放蕩息子アレックにレイプされ、私生児を産みます。男に捨てられ、乳農場で働く中に、真面目な青年エンジェルと恋仲になります。求婚されたテスは、自分の過去を告白しようとしますが、不運な偶然もあって、エンジェルは新婚旅行の夜初めてテスの過去を知ります。動揺した彼はブラジルへと去ります。

　アレックと再会した彼女は、家族の窮状を救うため彼の情婦になります。ブラジルでテスを許そうと決心したエンジェルが帰国します。追い詰められたテスは発作的にアレックを殺害します。エンジェルと共に逃亡、つかの間の幸福を味わった後、ストーンヘンジで官憲に捕えられ処刑されます。

　殺人を犯したテスですが、作者は「清純な女性」という副題をつけています。エンジェルへの愛を貫き、家族のために誠実に生きた彼女を肯定しているのは明白です。一方、女性の自我を無視した時代、男たちへの批判も明白です。ポランスキー監督の映画では 女優がテスの雰囲気をよく出しています。

Tess of the d'Urbervilles

(1) テスがエンジェルにプロポーズされ、喜びながらも、過去が気になる身なので、慎重に対応する場面です。

'If it is *sure* to make you happy to have me as your wife, and you feel that you do wish to marry me, *very, very* much—'
　'I do, dearest, of course!'
　'I mean, that it is only your wanting me very much, and being hardly able to keep alive without me, whatever my offences, that ₅ would make me feel I ought to say I will.'
　'You will—you do say it, I know! You will be mine for ever and ever.' →

Notes ●●●●●

1- **sure, very, very**　彼の愛情を慎重に確かめているので、強調のためイタリック体になっています。

4- **It is only ... that would ...**　ここも慎重です。It...that の強調文です。全体で「私に結婚しますと言うべきだと思わせるのは、私の罪がどのようなものであれ、あなたが私をとても欲し、私なしでは殆ど生きていけないという場合だけです」が直訳です。

5 **whatever my offences**　テスとしては、処女を失った事件を念頭に置いていますが、エンジェルは軽く、「ふつつかな者ですが」と言っているのだと解釈したでしょう。offence という単語自体は、どちらの解釈も可能です。

5- **that would make me feel**　仮定法の would が使われていますね。will の場合より、可能性が低いのです。「まあ、そういうことはないかもしれないのだが…」という気分なのです。ここでもつつましく、遠慮した心理が働いています。

Thomas Hardy

→ He clasped her close and kissed her.
'Yes!'
She had no sooner said it than she burst into a dry hard sobbing, so violent that it seemed to rend her. Tess was not a hysterical girl by any means, and he was surprised.
'Why do you cry, dearest?'
'I can't tell—quite!—I am so glad to think—of being yours, and making you happy!'
'But this does not seem very much like gladness, my Tessy!'
'I mean—I cry because I have broken down in my vow! I said I would die unmarried!'
'But, if you love me you would like me to be your husband?'
'Yes, yes, yes! But O, I sometimes wish I had never been born.'

(Ch. 31, pp. 254–55)

*N*otes ●●●●

11　**had no sooner than ...**「するや否や」
12　**rend her**「(悲嘆などが) 心を引き裂く」
13　**and he was surprised**　この and は「そして」、「それから」と言う意味でよいでしょうか。いいえ、「それ故」としましょう。
18　**broken down in my vow**「自分の誓いにおいて失敗した」

(2) ストーンヘンジまで逃げてきた二人ですが、やがてテスを追って、警官たちが現れます。

They all closed in with evident purpose. Her story then was true! Springing to his feet, he looked around for a weapon, loose stone, means of escape, anything. By this time the nearest man was upon him.

'It is no use, sir,' he said. 'There are sixteen of us on the Plain, and the whole country is reared.'

'Let her finish her sleep!' he implored in a whisper of the men as they gathered round.

When they saw where she lay, which they had not done till then, they showed no objection, and stood watching her, as still as the pillars around. →

*N*otes ●●●●

1 **They all closed in**「迫ってきた」they は警官たちです。
   Her story was true! 描出話法で、エンジェルの心理が描かれています。「テスの言ったことは本当だったんだな」[英文法ガイド 10-III] 参照。story とはアレックを殺害したと言う告白です。ここで初めて、本当だと気付いたのでしょうか。
2 **Springing to his feet**「立ち上がって」
   a weapon, loose stone ... 何か逃れる手段、地面からはがれている石でもなんでもいい、という感じです。
3- **was upon him**「彼の体に接触した」
5 **it is no use, sir**「無駄ですよ」この sir は目上の男性への敬称ではなく、強めです。
   The Plain ストーンヘンジ遺跡一帯の平原部。
6 **The whole country is reared**「国中で大騒ぎになっている」rear（方言）「騒がせる」
7 **finish her sleep** テスは疲れ果てて眠り込んでいるのです。
   implored in a whisper of the men「警官たちに小声で懇願した」in a whisper「ひそひそ声で」は挿入句です。
10- **as still as the pillars**「周囲の石の柱同様に静かに」

Thomas Hardy

→ He went to the stone and bent over her, holding one poor little hand; her breathing now was quick and small, like that of a lesser creature than a woman. All waited in the growing light, their faces and hands as if they were silvered, the remainder of their figures dark, the stones glistening green-gray, the Plain still a mass of shade. Soon the light was strong, and a ray shone upon her unconscious form, peering under her eyelids and waking her.

'What is it, Angel?' she said, starting up. 'Have they come for me?'

'Yes, dearest,' he said. 'They have come.'

'It is as it should be,' she murmured. 'Angel, I am almost glad—yes, glad! This happiness could not have lasted. It was too much. I have had enough; and now I shall not live for you to despise me!'

She stood up, shook herself, and went forward, neither of the men having moved.

'I am ready,' she said quietly. (Ch. 58, pp. 486–87)

Notes ●●●●●

13 **a lesser creature than a woman**「成人の女性より小さな生き物」子供でしょう。
14 **as if they were silvered**「あたかもそこだけ銀色に光っているかのように」
   the remainder ... ここは独立分詞構文で、being が省略されています。[英文法ガイド 5-II]参照。stones, Plain も同じ。
18 **What is it?** この it については、[英文法ガイド 11-4]参照。
   Starting up「飛び起きながら」
18– **come for me**「私を捕えに来た」
21 **It is as it should be**「物事はあるべきようになっている」が直訳。この it は What is it の it と同じです。「これでよいのだわ」と訳せます。
22 **This happiness could ...**「この幸福は長く続く筈がなかったわ」仮定法。「たとえ続くとしても」という if 節が省略。[英文法ガイド 9-IV-3]参照。
24 **shook herself**「服のちりを払った」

8.「ボヘミアの醜聞」
『シャーロック・ホームズの冒険』より

"A Scandal in Bohemia"
from The Adventures of Sherlock Holmes
(1892)
by
Conan Doyle

　コナン・ドイル Conan Doyle (1859–1930) は、近代推理小説の基礎を築いたイギリスの小説家。アイルランド人の両親からエディンバラで生まれました。親は貧乏でしたが、裕福な伯父の援助で土地の大学で医学を学び、開業しますが、成功せず、家計の足しにもと余暇に書いた推理小説『緋色の研究』(1887) が好評で、以後執筆に専念します。この長編に登場するロンドンのベイカー街221番地Bに住む素人探偵シャーロック・ホームズの抜群の推理力、綿密な観察力と相棒のワトソン博士の名コンビ振りが、世界中の推理小説愛好家を魅了することになりました。両人が活躍する長編として『バスカヴィル家の犬』(1902) も有名ですが、ドイル自身は歴史小説家として認められたいと望み、『マイカ・クラーク』他の歴史もの、さらに晩年には心霊術に魅せられ、『心霊術の歴史』(1926) などを書いています。

　シャーロック・ホームズとワトソン博士が登場するのは、『緋色の研究』などの4長編と56作からなる5冊の短編集です。『シャーロック・ホームズの冒険』 The Adventures of Sherlock Holmes (1892) は最初の短編集で12作収められています。本書ではその冒頭の短編「ボヘミアの醜聞」 "A Scandal in Bohemia" を読みます。ボヘミア国王が、ある国の王女と近く結婚することになったのですが、以前愛人であったオペラ歌手が、昔の王と自分との写真を王女に送ると脅迫してきます。ホームズは、国王から問題の写真を奪い取ることを依頼されます。変装したホームズは、密かに歌手の家に侵入して、写真の在りかを突き止めますが、同時に歌手もある男性と婚約中だということを発見。結局、写真は奪えなかったけれど、歌手が悪用しないと判明して、国王も納得し、一件解決します。

Conan Doyle

ワトソンがホームズを訪問すると、手紙で仕事を依頼してきた人物の代理人の伯爵がじきに到着するところでした。仮面をつけた人物が馬車で到着します。

'You had my note?' he asked with a deep harsh voice and a strongly marked German accent. 'I told you that I would call.' He looked from one to the other of us, as if uncertain which to address.
  'Pray take a seat,' said Holmes. 'This is my friend and colleague, Dr Watson, who is occasionally good enough to help me in my cases. Whom have I the honour to address?'
  'You may address me as the Count Von Kramm, a Bohemian nobleman. I understand that this gentleman, your friend, is a man of honour and discretion, whom I may trust with a matter of the most extreme importance. If not, I should much prefer to communicate with you alone.' →

Notes ●●●●
2 **strongly marked German accent**「とても強いドイツ語訛り」
3 **which to address**「どちらに話しかけるべきか」
6 **Whom have I the honour to address?**「誰に話しかける名誉を私は持つのか」が直訳で、What is your name? を大仰に言い換えたものです。
8– **a man of honour and discretion**「名誉心と慎重さを持ち合わせる人」
9 **trust＋人＋with＋物**「人に物を託す」

"A Scandal in Bohemia"

→ I rose to go, but Holmes caught me by the wrist and pushed me back into my chair. 'It is both, or none,' said he. 'You may say before this gentleman anything which you may say to me.'

The Count shrugged his broad shoulders. 'Then I must begin,' said he, 'by binding you both to absolute secrecy for two years, at the end of that time the matter will be of no importance. At present it is not too much to say that it is of such weight it may have an influence upon European history.'

'I promise,' said Holmes.

'And I.' →

Notes ● ● ● ●

12 **I rose to go**　このIはDr Watsonです。物語は博士の視点から書かれています。
　caught me by the wrist「私の手首をつかんだ」
13 **It is both, or none**　やや無理な表現ですが、文脈から「二人に任すか、それがいやなら、話がなかったことにしましょう」という意味。
16 **by binding you both to absolute secrecy**「絶対的な秘密厳守という誓約を二人にさせることによって、話を始めよう」というのは、「お二人とも、誓約願いたい」と命じることに等しいのです。
18 **It is not too much to say that**「～と言っても言い過ぎでない」

39

Conan Doyle

→ 'You will excuse this mask,' continued our strange visitor. 'The august person who employs me wishes his agent to be unknown to you, and I may confess at once that the title by which I have just called myself is not exactly my own.'

'I was aware of it,' said Holmes dryly.

'The circumstances are of great delicacy, and every precaution has to be taken to quench what might grow to be an immense scandal and seriously compromise one of the reigning families of Europe. To speak plainly, the matter implicates the great House of Ormstein, hereditary kings of Bohemia.'

'I was also aware of that,' murmured Holmes, settling himself down in his armchair, and closing his eyes. →

Notes ••••

22 **You will excuse this mask** この will は軽い命令です。
23 **august person**「お偉いお方」
 agent「代理人」
27 **of great delicacy**「この上なく微妙な」cf. of use = useful. 依頼人の大仰な物腰や物言いが、ホームズには多少とも滑稽に見えています。
27– **every precaution must be taken** take precaution「用心する、警戒する」
28 **quench**「(醜聞などを) 押さえつける、もみ消す」
 what might grow to be「なりかねないこと」この might は may より弱いのです。「ひょっとするとかもしれない」[英文法ガイド 9–IV–5] 参照。what がどこまで続くのでしょうか？ Europe までですよ。
29 **compromise**「～の評判を貶める」です。
30 **implicates** 犯罪や醜聞などに巻き込む、という意味です。
30– **the great House of Ormstein, hereditary kings of Bohemia**「ボヘミアの伝統ある王家、偉大なるオルムシュタイン家」

"A Scandal in Bohemia"

→ Our visitor glanced with some apparent surprise at the languid, lounging figure of the man who had been no doubt depicted to him as the most incisive reasoner, and most energetic agent in Europe. Holmes slowly reopened his eyes, and looked impatiently at his gigantic client.

'If your Majesty would condescend to state your case,' he remarked, 'I should be better able to advise you.'

The man sprang from his chair, and paced up and down the room in uncontrollable agitation. Then, with a gesture of desperation, he tore the mask from his face and hurled it upon the ground. 'You are right,' he cried; 'I am the King. Why should I attempt to conceal it?' (Ch. 1, pp. 14–15)

*N*otes ●●●●●

34– **languid, lounging figure**「けだるそうな、だらしない姿」世間一般の探偵とはかなり違うのですね！
35　**had been ... depicted**　これこれの人だと聞かされていた、というので、過去完了形ですから、ホームズに仕事を依頼する以前のことです。
36　**incisive reasoner**「頭脳明晰な推理家」
　　agent「秘密諜報員」ですが、ここでは「私立探偵」のこと。
38　**gigantic**　依頼人はとても巨漢なのです。
39　**condescend to state your case**　condescend to ~ というのは、身分の高い人が「高ぶらずに～する」と「偉そうな態度で～する」と相反する意味合いがあるので厄介です。ここではどっちでしょう？　そう、前者です。ホームズの発言だからです。「王様が事件のありのままをお話しくだされば、うまくご助言申しあげられましょうに」くらいの感じですね。[英文法ガイド 9-I-2, IV-5] 参照。
41　**sprang up**「飛び上がった」のは、ホームズが変装を見やぶったからです。
44　**Why should I ... ?**　これは修辞学上の疑問文ですね。「するべきか、否、そんなことはない」[英文法ガイド 10-II-2-C] 参照。

9.『ピグマリオン (マイ・フェア・レディ)』

Pygmalion
(1913)
by
George Bernard Shaw

　バーナード・ショー Bernard Shaw (1856–1950) は、アイランドの劇作家、評論家、教育家、ジャーナリストです。イギリス近代劇の始祖。だらしない父とインテリで音楽家の母との間にダブリンで生まれました。1876年にロンドンに渡り、イギリス労働党の前身である「ファビアン協会」の設立に関与し、政治的経済的な論文を多数執筆。イプセンの影響下で劇作を始め、1892年の処女作『男やもめの家』から1924年の『聖ジョーン』まで、社会の因習を批判する内容の劇を多数発表。1925年には、アイルランド人ではイェイツに次ぐ二人目となるノーベル文学賞を受賞。「他に類を見ない風刺に満ち、理想性と人間性を描いた作品を送りだした」というのが受賞理由でした。批評家としては、行き過ぎた資本主義を批判し、男女平等、社会改革、労働者の権利保護などを支持しました。教育者としては、自分自身は大学出でないのに、ロンドン・スクール・オブ・エコノミックスを創立した功績が目に付きます。日本でも、大正、昭和初期にはイギリス作家の中で大きな存在とみなされ、翻訳もいくつも出ました。昭和8年の来日時には、荒木貞夫陸軍大臣と戦争について対談して話題を呼びました。第二次大戦後も、高齢になっても衰えなかったショー翁の毒舌は日本の新聞でも報じられました。

　ロンドン下町の花売り娘イライザが、音声学者のヒギンズ教授と出会い、発音矯正から始まり、次第に女性としての自我に目覚め、自立してゆく姿を描いた劇です。ハリウッドで映画化され、『マイ・フェア・レディ』として有名になりました。原作のヒギンズは、著名な音声学者で気難しい独身男で、レックス・ハリソン演ずる明朗な教授とは違います。映画では、イライザは教授を捨てて、平等の人間として尊重してくれる青年を選びます。よく引き合いに出されるせりふの The rain in Spain stays mainly in the plain. は原作にはありません。

Pygmalion

(1) ヒギンズが発音練習を始めるにあたっての心構えをイライザに言い聞かせている場面。

HIGGINS. Eliza: you are to live here for the next six months, learning how to speak beautifully, like a lady in a florist's shop. If you're good and do whatever you're told, you shall sleep in a proper bedroom, and have lots to eat, and money to buy chocolates and take rides in taxis. If you're naughty and idle you will sleep in the back kitchen among the black beetles, and be walloped by Mrs. Pearce with a broomstick. At the end of six months you shall go to Buckingham Palace in a carriage, beautifully dressed. →

*N*otes ●●●●●

1 **You are to live here**「ここで暮らすことになった」be 動詞 + 不定詞の予定の用法です。[英文法ガイド 3-I-4] 参照。
2 **A lady in a florist's shop** 花屋で働く上品な女性。
3 **you shall sleep**「寝させてあげる」この shall は語り手の意志を示す、やや古風な用法。
7 **walloped** 口語で「殴られる」
8 **Buckingham Palace ...** ロンドンにある英国王室の宮殿。これは、もちろん例えばの話ですね。イライザを子供扱いし、話を大袈裟にしています。

→ If the King finds out you're not a lady, you will be taken by the police to the Tower of London, where your head will be cut off as a warning to other presumptuous flower girls. If you are not found out, you shall have a present of seven-and-sixpence to start life with as a lady in a shop. If you refuse this offer you will be a most ungrateful and wicked girl; and the angels will weep for you.

MRS. PEARCE [*patiently*] I think you'd better let me speak to the girl properly in private. I don't know that I can take charge of her or consent to the arrangement at all. Of course I know you don't mean her any harm; but when you get what you call interested in people's accents, you never think or care what may happen to them or you. Come with me, Eliza (Act II, pp. 45–46)

*N*otes ●●●●
10 **The Tower of London**　ロンドン塔。1952 年まで牢獄に使われていました。
12–　**seven-and-sixpence**「7 シリング 6 ペンス」1971 年以前の貨幣単位。
17　**in private**「二人だけで」家政婦はこんな話し方では、イライザに教授の趣旨がうまく伝わらないと知っています。
　　take charge of her「彼女の世話をする」
18–　**don't mean her any harm**「彼女に対して悪いことを意図するのでない」が直訳。第 4 文型。[英文法ガイド 1–IV] 参照。
19–　**get what you ... you**「先生は、いわゆる関心を抱くとなると、相手なりご自分なりがどうなろうと一切構わなくなってしまうのですからねえ」what you call「いわゆる」は、軽蔑、批判を暗示します。家政婦はヒギンズのやり方に困っているようです。その尻拭いを自分の役目だと割り切って諦めているようでもありますが。

Pygmalion

(2) 最後です。女性として自我に目覚めたイライザは、不満をぶちまけます。ヒギンズの女性蔑視に耐えられず、別の思いやりある青年を選んだようです。

LIZA. [*desperate*] Oh, you are a cruel tyrant. I can't talk to you: you turn everything against me: I'm always in the wrong. But you know very well all the time that you're nothing but a bully. You know I can't go back to the gutter, as you call it, and that I have no real friends in the world but you and the Colonel. You know well I couldn't bear to live with a low common man after you two; and it's wicked and cruel of you to insult me by pretending I could. You think I must go back to Wimpole Street because I have nowhere else to go but father's. But don't you be too sure that you have me under your feet to be trampled on and talked down. I'll marry Freddy, I will, as soon as I'm able to support him. (Act V, p. 37)

Notes ●●●●

1 **LIZA** Eliza と同じ。
   desperate 「やけくそになって」
1- **I can't talk ... against me** 「先生には何も言えないわ。だって、何を言っても意味を曲げて取るんだ。いつだって、私は間違っているっていうのよ」
3 **nothing but a bully** 「弱い者いじめに過ぎない」
4 **the gutter, as you call it** 「先生が言うところのドブの生活」
6 **couldn't bear** 「我慢しようとしても出来ないだろう」この couldn't は仮定法です。[英文法ガイド 9–IV–3] 参照。
7 **after you two** 「お二人のような紳士を知った後では」
   it's wicked and cruel of you to ~ 「~するなんて間違っているし意地悪よ」
8 **I could** 次に bear を補って考えること。
   Wimpole Street イライザの父の住む所。
9- **don't you be too sure** 「あまり自信を持ち過ぎちゃいけませんよ」
10- **You have me ... down** 「踏みつけ、言い負かすべく、私を先生の足下に確保している」が直訳です。
11- **as soon ... him** つまり結婚できる収入を稼げるようになり次第。

45

10.『雨』

Rain
(1921)
by
William Somerset Maugham

　サマセット・モーム Somerset Maugham (1874–1965) は、20世紀前半のイギリス文学を代表する小説家、劇作家。パリで生まれ、両親の死で孤児となり、イギリスで育ち、不幸な少年時代を送ります。パブリック・スクール途中でヨーロッパに遊学、帰国して医学校に入学、その経験に基づいて自然主義的な小説『ランベスのライザ』を発表、以後作家を目指します。風俗喜劇『フレデリック夫人』が商業的に大成功を収め「富のために魂を売った者」と批評家に酷評されますが、やがて純文学の自伝的な長編『人間の絆』を世に問い、さらに続くゴーギャンをモデルにした小説『月と六ペンス』、『お菓子とビール』、『剃刀の刃』などの数多くの長編、短編、『サミング・アップ』などのエッセイ、『ドン・フェルナンド』などの旅行記により、大衆からインテリまで幅広い読者を獲得。1959年に日本を訪問し歓迎されました。人間は矛盾した要素を内包する謎めいた存在だという人間不可知論を唱えました。

　マクフェイル医師は南海の島で1年間休養しようと妻と旅してきましたが、事件に巻き込まれます。伝染病が発生し中継地の宿で足止めされます。宿にはデイヴィッドソン宣教師夫妻のほか、ハワイから乗船した綺麗で下品なアメリカ娘ミス・トムソンがいます。毎晩ジャズを流して客を取っている様子で、宣教師は宿を淫売宿にすると言って怒り、島の総督を説得して、娘を強制送還させる命令を出させます。娘は、態度を一変して赦しを乞い、宣教師は、毎晩説教し彼女は別人のようになります。送還の前夜、宣教師は夜遅くまで女の部屋で過ごした後、翌朝、自殺した姿で発見されます。彼女は派手な態度に戻ります。「首尾一貫した人間など見たことがない」というモームの人間観が露わに出た作品として有名です。善と悪が混在しているのが人間の有様だと信じる作者ですから、宣教師と同じ矛盾した要素が全ての人間に存在すると知るべきだと、言いたいのでしょう。短編だけに映画化は全体としては原作をよく伝えています。

Rain

(1) 冒頭です。

It was nearly bed-time and when they awoke next morning land would be in sight. Dr Macphail lit his pipe and, leaning over the rail, searched the heavens for the Southern Cross. After two years at the front and a wound that had taken longer to heal than it should, he was glad to settle down quietly at Apia for twelve months at least, and he felt already better for the journey.

(*Complete Stories* I, Heinemann, p. 1)

Notes ●●●●●

1– **land would be in sight**「陸地が見えるだろう」船員らがそう言ったか、あるいは、知識のあるこの医師がそう思ったのか、どちらかです。この文の前に they said あるいは he thought を補って考えるといいです。
3 **searched the heavens for ~**「~を求めて空を探した」
4 **the front**「前線」
4– **taken longer to heal than it should**「治癒するのに、通常かかる期間よりも長く要した」should の後に heal が省略。
5 **Apia**　南海サモア諸島のウポル島の首府。
6 **for the journey**「旅に出たというだけで」

William Somerset Maugham

(2) ミス・トムソンに同情した医師が、宣教師に強引すぎると抗議する場面。デイヴィッドスンは「義務を果たすのみです」と言い張ります。

　"I don't see that it can make any difference if she goes to Sydney rather than to San Francisco, and so long as she promises to behave while she's here it's dashed hard to persecute her."
　The missionary fixed him with his stern eyes.
　"Why is she unwilling to go back to San Francisco?" 5
　"I didn't enquire," answered the doctor with some asperity. "And I think one does better to mind one's own business."
　Perhaps it was not a very tactful answer.
　"The governor has ordered her to be deported by the first boat that leaves the island. He's only done his duty and I will not inter- 10 fere. Her presence is a peril here."
　"I think you're very harsh and tyrannical."
　The two ladies looked up at the doctor with some alarm, but they need not have feared a quarrel, for the missionary smiled gently.
　"I'm terribly sorry you should think that of me, Dr Macphail. 15 Believe me, my heart bleeds for that unfortunate woman, but I'm only trying to do my duty." (p. 26)

*N*otes ●●●●

1　**it can make ... to Sydney**「シドニーに行けば何か差異が生じうる（とは思わない）」it は if 以下、つまり「行くかどうか」を指します。
2　**behave**「行儀よく振る舞う」
3　**dashed hard**　dashed は口語、俗語で damned と同じで、強めです。
6　**asperity**「荒々しさ、痛切さ」
6–　**And I think**　この and は、文の冒頭に置かれているので、強調を表します。
7　**one does better to mind one's own business**「他人事に口出ししないほうがいい」気取った意味合いの one です。[英文法ガイド 11-2, 3] 参照。
8　**tactful**「巧みな」
9　**deported**「退去させられる」
15　**should think that of me**「私のことをそう思うなんて」という感じです。

(3) 最後の場面。宣教師の自殺後、ミス・トムソンは元に戻ります。非難するマクフェイル医師に向かって、彼女は乱暴な言葉を吐き、事情が明白になります。

　　Miss Thompson was standing at her door, chatting with a sailor. A sudden change had taken place in her. She was no longer the cowed drudge of the last days. She was dressed in all her finery, in her white dress, with the high shiny boots over which her fat legs bulged in their cotton stockings; her hair was elaborately arranged;　5 and she wore that enormous hat covered with gaudy flowers. Her face was painted, her eyebrows were boldly black, and her lips were scarlet. She held herself erect. She was the flaunting quean that they had known at first. As they came in she broke into a loud, jeering laugh; and then, when Mrs Davidson involuntarily stopped,　10 she collected the spittle in her mouth and spat. →

*N*otes ●●●●●

3　**cowed drudge**「怯えた奴隷みたいな女」
　dressed in all her finery「すっかり着飾って」このように総括的に述べてから、次に具体的な描写を行っています。数行下の Her face was painted も同じ書き方ですね。
8　**flaunting quean**「魅力をこれ見よがしに示すあばずれの女」が直訳です。quean（古風）「あばずれ女」
9　**they had known at first**　ここで注意すべきなのは、at first が first とか in the beginning と違って、後に変化した場合にのみ用いるということです。例えば、I was happy at first, but very unhappy after a week.
　broke into「〜を突然始めた」
11　**collected the spittle**「つばをためた」

William Somerset Maugham

→ Mrs Davidson cowered back, and two red spots rose suddenly to her cheeks. Then, covering her face with her hands, she broke away and ran quickly up the stairs. Dr Macphail was outraged. He pushed past the woman into her room.

"What the devil are you doing?" he cried. "Stop that damned machine."

He went up to it and tore the record off. She turned on him.

"Say, doc, you can that stuff with me. What the hell are you doin' in my room?"

"What do you mean?" he cried. "What d'you mean?"

She gathered herself together. No one could describe the scorn of her expression or the contemptuous hatred she put into her answer.

"You men! You filthy, dirty pigs! You're all the same, all of you. Pigs! Pigs!" (p. 38)

Notes ●●●●

12 **red spots rose**「赤い斑点が生じた」赤面したのです。
13 **broke away** = escaped.
14– **pushed past the woman into the room**「女を押しのけて部屋に入った」past は前置詞。
16 **What the devil are you doing?** the devil は強め。
16– **damned machine**「いまいましい機械」蓄音機のこと。腹立っているので、下品な言葉使いになり damned と言ったのです。
18 **turned on**「立ち向かった」
19 **you can that stuff with me**「わたし対してそんな変なことをするのは止めなよ」命令文の you がつくと、強調されます。can は俗語で「止める」と言う意味の動詞。stuff は口語で「下らぬこと」
22 **gathered herself together**「勇気を奮い起こした」
No one could describe「～を描写することは、仮にやろうとしたって、誰にも出来ないだろう」[英文法ガイド 9–IV–3] 参照。

11.『インドへの道』

A Passage to India
(1924)
by
E. M. Forster

　E. M. フォースター E. M. Forster (1879–1970) は、20世紀イギリス文学の寡作ながら代表的な小説家です。日本での知名度が低かったのですが、優れた映画化のせいで、知られるようになりました。裕福な家に生まれたのですが、建築家の父は2歳になる前に亡くなり、画家の母に養育されました。パブリック・スクールを経てケンブリッジ大学を卒業。イタリア、ギリシャを旅行し、次第に創作活動を始めました。イタリアが主な舞台の『眺めのいい部屋』、自伝的な『いと長き旅路』、教養と実務の対立・和解を描く『ハワーズ・エンド』などの小説を刊行。第一次大戦中はエジプトの赤十字で働き、さらにインドで長期滞在し、さらに藩主の秘書としても滞在。インドでの経験を生かしたのが、『インドへの道』です。第二次大戦が近づくと、民主主義擁護のための発言を忍耐強く続け、尊敬を得ました。没後、同性愛の性癖が公になりました。

　イギリス植民地時代のインドを舞台にして、現地人とイギリス人との対立を描いた小説。作者の関心は、政治的な分析にあるのでなく、人間同士の魂と魂との結びつきの可能性を追求することでした。今日でも、作品の価値は損なわれていません。ムア夫人は、インドの裁判所で働く息子の婚約者アデラと共に、息子を訪ねます。2人は、インドの青年医師アジズと知り合い、マラバー洞窟に案内されますが、洞窟内でアデラはアジズにレイプされたと思い込みます。人種間の憎悪は収拾がつかなくなり、裁判は異様な興奮に包まれます。アデラは、レイプは自分の錯覚だと証言します。洞窟でムア夫人が覚える虚無感を通じて、以前の小説では隠れたていたフォースターのペシミスティックな面が濃厚に出ていることにも注目するといいでしょう。そういう世界認識を根底に秘めつつ、なお人間同士の魂の結合の必要性を説き、正しい生き方を求めてやまない姿勢、これがフォースターの本質です。リーン監督の映画は、原作を部分的には忠実に再現しています。

E. M. Forster

(1) 三人で会話している場面。アデラとムア夫人対ロニーのインド人への態度の差が鮮明に出ます。

'This sounds very romantic,' said Miss Quested, who was exceedingly fond of Mrs Moore, and was glad she should have had this little escapade. 'You meet a young man in a mosque, and then never let me know!'

'I was going to tell you, Adela, but something changed the conversation and I forgot. My memory grows deplorable.'

'Was he nice?'

She paused, then said emphatically: 'Very nice.'

'Who was he?' Ronny enquired.

'A doctor. I don't know his name.'

'A doctor? I know of no young doctor in Chandrapore. How odd! What was he like?' →

Notes ●●●●

2- **was glad she should have ... escapade**「夫人がこの一寸した冒険をよくぞしたのを喜んだ」should は意外性を表します。

3- **You meet ... let me know**「回教寺院で青年に出会ったくせに、私に黙っていたなんて！」という感じです。現在形を使っていますね。過去の事柄をあたかも目前の出来事のように伝える「劇的現在、歴史的現在」の用法です。

8 **She posed** ムア夫人はよく考えてから物を言っていますね。

11 **I know of no young doctor**「若い医者は一人も知らない」
Chandrapore 架空の町。作者が知っている町がモデルです。

'Rather small, with a little moustache and quick eyes. He called out to me when I was in the dark part of the mosque—about my shoes. That was how we began talking. He was afraid I had them on, but I remembered luckily. He told me about his children, and then we walked back to the club. He knows you well.'

'I wish you had pointed him out to me. I can't make out who he is.'

'He didn't come into the club. He said he wasn't allowed to.'

Thereupon the truth struck him, and he cried, 'Oh, good gracious! Not a Mohammedan? Why ever didn't you tell me you'd been talking to a native? I was going all wrong.' (Ch. 3, pp. 23–24)

*N*otes ●●●●●

16 **I remembered** 目的語は書いてありませんが、to take off one's shoes が省略されています。remember to ~「忘れずに～する」
18 **wish you had pointed him out**「あの人だと指摘してくれたらよかったのに」実際はそうしなかったのです。[英文法ガイド 9–IV–1] 参照。
21 **the truth struck him**「真相が頭に浮かんだ」
   good gracious「何ていうことだ」驚きの感嘆詞。
22 **Not a Mohammedan?**「まさか回教徒じゃあないのでしょ?」
23 **going all wrong**「すっかり勘違いして」

E. M. Forster

(2) 裁判の場面で、アデラの告訴取り消しで大騒ぎが生じます。

 'What is that, what are you saying? Speak up, please.' The Magistrate bent forward.
 'I'm afraid I have made a mistake.'
 'What nature of mistake?'
 'Dr Aziz never followed me into the cave.' 5
 The Superintendent slammed down his papers, then picked them up and said calmly: 'Now, Miss Quested, let us go on. I will read you the words of the deposition which you signed two hours later in my bungalow.'
 'Excuse me, Mr McBryde, you cannot go on. I am speaking to 10 the witness myself. And the public will be silent. If it continues to talk, I have the court cleared. Miss Quested, address your remarks to me, who am the Magistrate in charge of the case, and realize their extreme gravity. Remember you speak on oath, Miss Quested.' →

*N*otes ●●●●

1 **Speak up**「声を高めてはっきり言って下さい」
2 **Magistrate**「裁判官」ここではインド人です。
6 **Superintendent**「警察部長」検事側で論告をします。イギリス人でMcBryde という名前。
 slammed down his papers「書類を机に叩きつけた」
8 **deposition**「宣誓証言」
12 **I have the court cleared**「法廷から全員退去を命ずる」
13 **in charge of the case**「当該事件担当の判事」
13– **their extreme gravity**「その極度の重大性」their は her remarks を指す。
14 **you speak on oath**「宣誓した上での発言ですよ」

A Passage to India

→ 'Dr Aziz never—'

'I stop these proceedings on medical grounds,' cried the Major on a word from Turton, and all the English rose from their chairs at once, large white figures behind which the little magistrate was hidden. The Indians rose too, hundreds of things went on at once, so that afterwards each person gave a different account of the catastrophe.

'You withdraw the charge? Answer me,' shrieked the representative of Justice. (Ch. 24, pp. 203–04)

Notes ●●●●●

16– **The Major on a word from Turton**「タートンから一言いわれて」Major はイギリス人の医務長官で病院長。Turton はこの地域の最高権力者の地方長官。
18　**large white figures**　前の all the English と同格です。
21　**catastrophe**「破局」混乱状態で終わった裁判のこと。
22　**You withdraw the charge**「告訴を取り下げるのですね？」アデラへの質問。
22– **representative of Justice**「正義の代表」とは Magistrate「裁判長」の言い換えです。

12.『チャタレイ夫人の恋人』

Lady Chatterley's Lover
(1928)
by
D. H. Lawrence

　D. H. ロレンス D. H. Lawrence (1885–1930)　20世紀のイギリス小説家として大きな存在。炭坑夫頭を父として生まれました。母は元教師のインテリでしたから、階級や教養の差のために、母は夫を無視し息子たちを溺愛。ロレンスの女性関係が歪んだ一因でした。奨学金で大学入学し、卒業後、教員をしながら、執筆開始。恩師の妻でドイツ貴族の娘フリーダを知り、ドイツへ駆け落ち。以後、世間の俗習や貧困に悩みながら、ヨーロッパ各地、アメリカ、メキシコなどを転々とし、45歳の時、南仏で病死するまでに、『息子と恋人』、『恋する女たち』、『チャタレー夫人の恋人』などの力作を刊行。現代文明の病弊の原因を人間のエゴイズムと肉体への不当な軽視の中に見て、エゴイズムに徹した人間同士の結びつき、とりわけ男女の結びつきの問題に取り組みました。

　富裕な画家を父とするコンスタンスは、大地主で気位の高い準男爵チャタレーと結婚しますが、夫は従軍し負傷して下半身不随で帰国。夫は世継ぎの必要から、妻の浮気を促します。彼女は夫の友人の画家などと肉体交渉しますが、満足できません。森番のメラーズと知り合い愛し合うようになり、精神、肉体の両面で満たされます。この小説の初版はイタリアで私家版で出ましたが、英米では、露骨な性描写の故に削除版しか出ませんでした。無削除版の刊行は、作者没後30年を経た1960年でした。刊行したペンギンブックス社は、起訴されたのですが、無罪。日本でも1950年に無削除版が出ると、警察にわいせつ文書と認定され、出版人と訳者が訴えられ、「チャタレー裁判」として今日でも記憶されています。作者は極めて真面目で、男女が自我を保ちつつ、優しさと思いやりをもって結合する理想の姿を追求しました。ファックやカントという語もそういう文脈では自然だと受け入れられます。中・上流階級の偽善や階級意識へ批判にも注目。映画では原作における議論より、性的な場面が強調されるのは仕方ないでしょう。

Lady Chatterley's Lover

(1) 書き出しです。夫妻の新婚から今に至る歴史が簡潔に語られています。

Ours is essentially a tragic age, so we refuse to take it tragically. The cataclysm has happened, we are among the ruins, we start to build up new little habitats, to have new little hopes. It is rather hard work: there is now no smooth road into the future: but we go round, or scramble over the obstacles. We've got to live, no matter 5 how many skies have fallen.

This was more or less Constance Chatterley's position. The war had brought the roof down over her head. And she had realized that one must live and learn. →

Notes •••••
1 **Ours is essentially a tragic age** チャタレー裁判でよく引用された箇所。「我々の時代は悲劇的なものである」弁護側は、このような知的な言説で始まる猥褻文学などあるだろうか、と問いかけました。しかし、ここはチャタレー夫人の思いを述べた言葉です。「今は本質的に悲劇的な時代ね。だからこそ悲劇的に取るのは嫌だわ」とでも訳すのが正確です。
2 **cataclysm**「大変動」
3 **habitats**「生息地」
4– **go round ... obstacles**「障害物を避けてぐるっと回ったり、その上を乗り越えていったりする」
5– **no matter how many skies have fallen**「いくら激変があったにしても」
7 **Constance Chatterley's position**「コンスタンス・チャタレーの見解」
8 **had brought ... head**「戦争で頭の上から屋根が落ちてきた」ひどい目にあったということ。
9 **live and learn** 諺で「生きていれば、いろいろと学べる」と言う意味です。

D. H. Lawrence

→ She married Clifford Chatterley in 1917, when he was home for a month on leave. They had a month's honeymoon. Then he went back to Flanders. To be shipped over to England again six months later, more or less in bits. Constance, his wife, was then twenty-three years old, and he was twenty-nine.

His hold on life was marvellous. He didn't die and the bits seemed to grow together again. For two years he remained in the doctor's hands. Then he was pronounced a cure, and could return to life again, with the lower half of his body, from the hips down, paralysed for ever. (Ch. 1, p. 5)

Notes ●●●●

11　**on leave**「休暇で」
12　**Flanders**「フランドル」第一次大戦の激戦地。
　　to be shipped　結果を表す不定詞。［英文法ガイド 3-I-3］参照。
13　**in bits**「かけらになって」身体中負傷して、を言い換えたもの。
15　**hold on life**「命にしがみ付く迫力」生命力と同じ。
15-　**bits seemed to grow together**　かけらが合体して育ったようだ、ということ。
17　**pronounced a cure**「治癒したと断言された」医者に、です。
18-　**with the lower ... for ever**　結局性的な機能が失われた状態になった、ということです。

Lady Chatterley's Lover

(2) 夫人は、メラーズと結ばれた後も、満足を得るための条件を話し合います。

"And you talk so coldly about sex," she said. "You talk as if you had only wanted your own pleasure and satisfaction."

She was protesting nervously against him.

"Nay!" he said. "I wanted to have my pleasure and satisfaction of a woman, and I never got it: because I could never get my pleasure and satisfaction of *her* unless she got hers of me at the same time. And it never happened. It takes two."

"But you never believed in your women. You don't even believe really in me," she said.

"I don't know what believing in a woman means."

"That's it, you see!"

She still was curled on his lap. But his spirit was grey and absent, he was not there for her. And everything she said drove him further.

→

Notes ●●●●●

4 **Nay** これは No と同じですが、地方語です。

4– **have my pleasure ... of a woman**「女性から喜びと満足を得る」メラーズには不仲の妻がいますし、過去には数名の女性がいました。その経験に言及しているのです。

6 **got hers of me**「おれから彼女の喜びを得た」

7 **it takes two**「(満足が得られるためには、性行為の成功には) 男女の双方が喜ぶことが必要だ」

11 **That's it, you see**「そらご覧なさい」やはり女を信じないのね、ということ。

12 **was curled on his lap**「彼の膝の上に体を丸くしていた」

13 **he was not there for her**「彼女に関心を全く示さなかった」
   drove him further「彼をさらに遠くに追いやった」

D. H. Lawrence

→ "But what *do* you believe in?" she insisted.
"I don't know."
"Nothing, like all the men I've ever known," she said.
They were both silent. Then he roused himself and said:
"Yes, I do believe in something. I believe in being warm-hearted. I believe especially in being warm-hearted in love, in fucking with a warm heart. I believe if men could fuck with warm hearts, and the women take it warm-heartedly, everything would come all right. It's all this cold-hearted fucking that is death and idiocy."
"But you don't fuck me cold-heartedly," she protested.
"I don't want to fuck you at all. My heart's as cold as cold potatoes just now."
"Oh!" she said, kissing him mockingly, "Let's have them *sauté*."
He laughed, and sat erect. (Ch. 14, pp. 206–07)

*N*otes ●●●●●
16 **Nothing**「何も信じないのね」
19 **being warm-hearted in love**「性行為の時に温かい心を持つこと」数行上で彼が言った、性の満足を得るための条件の言い換えとも言えますね。なお、この love はセックスのことです。Cf. make love「セックスする」
20– **if men could fuck ... all right**　ここは仮定法過去ですね。ということは、現在、実際にはそれがなされていないということです。[英文法ガイド 9–I] 参照。
22 **idiocy**「愚劣」
26 **Let's have them *sauté***「それを炒めて食べましょう」saute は元来フランス語で「炒め料理」ここは複数形。こうして二人は理想的な性行為をして、現代という悲劇的な時代を何とか生きて行くわけです。

Part 2

アメリカ文学編

1.『モヒカン族の最後』

The Last of the Mohicans
(1826)
by
James Fenimore Cooper

　ジェイムズ・フェニモア・クーパー James Fenimore Cooper (1789–1851) はニュージャージー州バーリントンの旧家に生まれ、ニューヨーク州西部で少年時代を過ごします。イエール大学に入りますが、放校処分を受けたために商船の船員、後には海軍軍人となります。結婚して退役、地主としての生活に入りましたが、家庭小説や、海上での生活をもとにした海洋小説を書き始めます。代表作は『レザーストッキング（革脚絆）物語』五部作で、いわば西部劇の元祖というべき物語です。主人公は「高貴な野蛮人」として描かれるナティ・バンポーという白人で、有名な開拓者ダニエル・ブーンがモデルであるとされ、文明社会より荒野を好む人物です。ある意味でアメリカ人の夢であり、神話、叙事詩とも言えるでしょう。アメリカ独立前後から西部の発展という激動の時代を背景として、失われる自然と消えゆく先住民族への郷愁を秘めたロマンティックな冒険物語です。作品はクーパーの生前から広く読まれて「アメリカのスコット」と称され、また文学史的には「アメリカ小説の父」という名誉ある地位を占める作家です。アメリカ独自の文学主題に最初に取り組んだからです。

　『モヒカン族の最後』は連作五編のうちの二作目です。一作目の『開拓者』で初老の人物として初登場した主人公がここでは三十代の半ばで、ホークアイ（鷹の目）と呼ばれています。イギリス軍のダンカン・ヘイワード少佐がモンロー大佐の二人の娘アリスとコーラを護衛して大佐の砦に向かいますが、案内人マグワの裏切りで危険に陥り、それを救うのがホークアイと、モヒカン族の族長チンガチグークです。その後も苦難は続き、チンガチグークの一人息子アンカスとコーラが命を落とし、ホークアイとチンガチグークはさらに奥地に進むというストーリーで、内容を考えるとこの小説は『モヒカン族最後の者』あるいは『最後のモヒカン族』とするのがふさわしいかもしれません。

　何度か映画化されていますが、1992 年の作品は大ヒットしました。雄大な森のシーンに始まり、音楽も魅力的です。

James Fenimore Cooper

(1) 第三章からの引用で、モヒカン族のチンガチグックとホークアイの会話です。

"My tribe is the grandfather of nations, but I am an unmixed man. The blood of chiefs is in my veins, where it must stay for ever. The Dutch landed, and gave my people the fire-water; they drank until the heavens and the earth seemed to meet, and they foolishly thought they had found the Great Spirit. Then they parted with their land. Foot by foot, they were driven back from the shores, until I, that am a chief and a Sagamore, have never seen the sun shine but through the trees, and have never visited the graves of my fathers."

→

Notes ●●●●●

1 **My tribe** モヒカン族のこと。
grandfather「始祖、祖先」
unmixed「純粋な」混血していないというのですね。動物でも「純血種」という言葉があります。
3 **fire-water**「強い酒、火酒」
they = my people.
3– **drank until ... meet**「天と地が合体するかに思えるまで」つまり泥酔した状態です。
5 **the Great Spirit**「(北米先住民の宗教の) 大霊、主神、守護神」
6 **Foot by foot**「一歩また一歩と」
driven back from the shores「(東部の) 海岸から (西の内陸へと) 追いやられた」
7 **Sagamore**「(ニューイングランド地方の先住民の) 族長」
7– **have never ... trees**「木々の間を通してしか太陽を見ていない」とは森林で暮らすからです。but = except.

The Last of the Mohicans

→ "Graves bring solemn feelings over the mind," returned the scout, a good deal touched at the calm suffering of his companion; "and they often aid a man in his good intentions, though, for myself, I expect to leave my own bones unburied, to bleach in the woods, or to be torn asunder by the wolves. But where are to be found those of your race who came to their kin in the Delaware country, so many summers since?"

"Where are the blossoms of those summers!—fallen, one by one: so all of my family departed, each in his turn, to the land of spirits. I am on the hill-top, and must go down into the valley; and when Uncas follows in my footsteps, there will no longer be any of the blood of the Sagamores, for my boy is the last of the Mohicans." (State University of New York Press, Ch. 3, p. 33)

*N*otes ●●●●●

10   **scout**「監視者」ホークアイを指します。
     a good deal touched「大いに感動して」touched の前に being が省略されています。[英文法ガイド 5-I-1] 参照。
12- **to bleach ... wolves**「森で白骨化し、狼に八つ裂きにされるべく」結果を表わす不定詞。[英文法ガイド 3-I-3] 参照。
13- **where are to be found**「見つけられるのか」この不定詞は可能を表わします。文の主語は those 以下です。those = graves.
14   **Delaware**「デラウェア」
15   **since** = ago.
16   **where are ... summers**「過去の夏の花の行く末はどこであろうか、先祖の墓もそれと同じだ」という意味合いです。
19   **Uncas**「アンカス」チンガチグックの息子。

James Fenimore Cooper

(2) 物語の最後、死んだアンカスの墓で嘆いている場面です。

　"No, no," cried Hawk-eye, who had been gazing with a yearning look at the rigid features of his friend, with something like his own self-command, but whose philosophy could endure no longer; "no, Sagamore, not alone. The gifts of our colours may be different, but God has so placed us as to journey in the same path. I have no kin, and I may also say, like you, no people. He was your son, and a red-skin by nature; and it may be, that your blood was nearer;—but if ever I forget the lad, who has so often fou't at my side in war, and slept at my side in peace, may He who made us all, whatever may be our colour or our gifts, forget me. The boy has left us for a time, but, Sagamore, you are not alone!" →

Notes ●●●●

1　**Hawk-eye**　「ホークアイ」鷹の目という意味で、主人公の別名。
2　**features**　目鼻立ちなど、顔の造作を指します。「顔つき、容貌」場合によっては「顔」です。
　　his friend　チンガチグックを指します。
2-　**something like his own self-command**　「自分自身の克己心に似たあるもの」が直訳。
3　**whose philosophy ... longer**　「その諦念がもはや持続できなかった」
4　**our colours**　肌の色のことです。
5　**so placed us as to ~**　「我々が〜するように配置された」
6　**no people**　「同じ部族の者」の意味の people です。
7　**by nature**　「生まれつき」
　　it may be, that ~　「〜かもしれない」今の英語なら、コンマはないのが普通。
　　your blood was nearer　親子だから血筋は私より近い、ということ。
8-　**if I ... forget me**　「万一私が彼を忘れるようなことがあれば、(神様に贈られた肌の色の相違がどうであれ、我々全人を創造された) 神様が私をお忘れになってもよい」神様が私を忘れることが絶対にないように、私も彼を決して忘れません、ということ。

The Last of the Mohicans

→ Chingachgook grasped the hand that, in the warmth of feeling, the scout had stretched across the fresh earth, and in that attitude of friendship, these two sturdy and intrepid woodsmen bowed their heads together, while scalding tears fell to their feet, watering the grave of Uncas, like drops of falling rain.

In the midst of the awful stillness with which such a burst of feeling, coming, as it did, from the two most renowned warriors of that region, was received, Tamenund lifted his voice, to disperse the multitude.

"It is enough!" he said. "Go, children of the Lenape; the anger of the Manitto is not done. Why should Tamenund stay? The pale-faces are masters of the earth, and the time of the red-men has not yet come again. My day has been too long. In the morning I saw the sons of Unamis happy and strong; and yet, before the night has come, have I lived to see the last warrior of the wise race of the Mohicans!" (Ch. 33, pp. 349–50)

*N*otes ●●●●

13 **the fresh earth** 遺体を埋めたばかりだから、「掘ったばかりの土」なのです。
14 **intrepid**「勇敢な」
15 **scalding tears**「熱い涙」scalding = very hot, burning.
17 **with which ~**「静寂は~によって迎えられた」［英文法ガイド 8-I-3］参照。
18 **coming, as it did, from ~**「(感情の発作は) 実際、~から出たものだったので」勇猛な戦士はめったに涙を見せないことになっていたのに、ここでは激しく泣いたので、周囲の者たちはしんと静まりかえっていたのです。
19 **Tamenund**「タメヌンド」デラウェアインディアンの酋長で友好的な人物。Tamanend, Tammany とも呼ばれています。／ 21 **Lenape** = Delaware.
22 **Manitto**「マニート」先住民が信じていた神あるいは霊。
  Why should Tamenund stay?「わしも留まるべきだろうか、いや、そうではない」修辞疑問です。［英文法ガイド 10-II-2-C］参照。
22- **pale-faces** 白人のこと。
24 **My day has been too long** この日のことではなく、自分の生涯について述べています。次の「朝」も昔を指します。／ 25 **Unamis**「ウナミ族」
26- **have I lived ... Mohicans**「長生きして、賢明な種族モヒカン族最後の戦士を見ることになった」

2.『アッシャー家の崩壊』

The Fall of the House of Usher
(1839)
by
Edgar Allan Poe

　エドガー・アラン・ポオ Edgar Allan Poe (1809–49) アメリカの詩人、短編作家。役者の両親から生まれますが、幼児のとき両親を亡くし、富裕な商人アラン夫妻に育てられます。ヴァージニア大学で学びますが、酒と賭博で負債を作り、家を出て、軍隊に入ったのですが、以前から詩集を出していたので、文筆で身を立てようと、退役。伯母の家に身を寄せ 13 歳の従妹と結婚。伯母と 3 人で幸福な生活を味わい、雑誌に短編と詩をいくつも発表し編集者としても手腕を発揮します。それでも貧困から抜け出せず、飲酒に耽りました。愛妻が突然喀血し、亡くなるまでの 5 年間、悲惨な生活を余儀なくされ、彼は不遇を嘆き絶望し、酒乱になりました。妻が亡くなると、妻に代わる女性を求め狂ったような生活をします。最期は、路上で行き倒れとなって発見されます。詩作では、天上の美、幽玄な美をメランコリックに歌った「大鴉」「アナベル・リー」などが有名です。言葉は音楽と結びついて霊妙な美を生み出す、という彼の説は、フランスの象徴詩人に影響を与え、ボードレールやマラルメが彼を論評し翻訳して世界中に知らしめることになりました。

　これは、謎めいて怪奇なゴチック風の短編代表作で、何度も映画化されています。陰鬱な沼の隣に立つ、不吉な雰囲気のアッシャー館（やかた）で展開する奇怪な話。一家の若い当主ロデリックの懇請で訪問した私は、友人の心身ともに衰弱した様子に心を痛めます。最愛の妹マデラインも正体不明の病気です。その妹が遂に息絶えたと聞き、二人で地下の棺に納めます。しかし、ある夜彼女は血だらけの経帷子の姿で現れ、兄にもたれかかり、兄妹は同時に死亡します。目撃した私は館から逃げますが、振り返ると、館が真二つに裂けて崩壊し、沼の中に消えて行きました。怪奇で凄惨な話なのに、どこか美的な快感、甘美な憂愁を覚えるのは不思議です。映画化はエプスタン監督の無声映画『アッシャー家の末裔』も一見の価値あり。

The Fall of the House of Usher

(1) 書き出しです。この邸が外観だけでもいかに沈鬱なものか、描写が的確です。

 During the whole of a dull, dark, and soundless day in the autumn of the year, when the clouds hung oppressively low in the heavens, I had been passing alone, on horseback, through a singularly dreary tract of country; and at length found myself, as the shades of the evening drew on, within view of the melancholy House of Usher. I know not how it was—but, with the first glimpse of the building, a sense of insufferable gloom pervaded my spirit. I say insufferable; for the feeling was unrelieved by any of that half-pleasureable, because of poetic, sentiment, with which the mind usually receives even the sternest natural images of the desolate or terrible. →

Notes ●●●●●

- 2– **the clouds hung oppressively low in the heavens**「空で雲が重苦しく低く垂れさがっていた」
- 4 **tract of country**「地域」
- 5 **within view of**「〜の見えるところに」
- 6 **know not** = don't know. 古風な表現。
- 7 **insufferable gloom pervaded my spirit**「やり切れぬ憂鬱が心に沁み渡った」
- 8 **unrelieved**「軽減されない」
- 9 **half-pleasurable, because of poetic, sentiment**「詩的であるため半ば快い情念」
- 10 **the sternest natural images of the desolate or terrible**「荒涼あるいは荘厳な事物が示すこの上なく厳しい自然の姿」この邸と険しい峡谷などを見る場合との違いに言及しています。

Edgar Allan Poe

→ I looked upon the scene before me—upon the mere house, and the simple landscape features of the domain, upon the bleak walls, upon the vacant eye-like windows, upon a few rank sedges, and upon a few white trunks of decayed trees—with an utter depression of soul which I can compare to no earthly sensation more properly than to the after-dream of the reveller upon opium: the bitter lapse into everyday life, the hideous dropping off of the veil. There was an iciness, a sinking, a sickening of the heart, an unredeemed dreariness of thought which no goading of the imagination could torture into aught of the sublime.

(*Penguin Book of American Short Stories*, p. 56)

Notes ●●●●

- 12 **landscape features of the domain**「地域の風景をなす事物の数々」
- 13 **rank sedges**「繁茂するツゲ」
- 14– **with an utter depression of soul**「まったく滅入った気分で」上の looked にかかります。
- 15 **earthly sensation**「この世の感覚」
- 16 **after-dream of the reveller upon opium**「アヘン吸引者の陶酔から醒めた後の白けた、酔いざめ心地」以下の二つの同格の句は言い換えです。
- 17 **the bitter lapse**「悲しい逆戻り」
- 17– **the hideous dropping of the veil**「夢の帳 (とばり) が消えるぞっとする気持」
- 18 **an iciness, a sinking ... heart**「胸が冷え冷えし沈み込み吐き気がする感覚」
- 19– **no goading ... sublime**「どう想像力を掻き立てようとも、何か崇高なものであると曲解するのは不可能だった」torture「捻じ曲げる、こじつける」

The Fall of the House of Usher

(2) ロデリックは妹マデラインについて、早すぎた埋葬をしたと告白します。

'Not hear it?—yes, I hear it, and *have* heard it. Long—long—long—many minutes, many hours, many days, have I heard it—yet I dared not—oh, pity me, miserable wretch that I am!—I dared not—I *dared* not speak! *We have put her living in the tomb!* Said I not that my senses were acute? I *now* tell you that I heard her first feeble movements in the hollow coffin. I heard them—many, many days ago—yet I dared not—*I dared not speak!*' (p. 73)

Notes •••••
1 **Not hear it?** = Don't I hear it?　it は地下の遺体安置所から聞こえてくる物音。
3 **dared not**「勇気がなかった」
  miserable wretch that I am　全体が直前の me と同格です。「勇気に欠けるだらしない男」ということ。
5 **my senses were acute**　感覚が鋭いので、小さな物音でも、君よりずっと早く聞き取れた、と告白するのです。

Edgar Allan Poe

(3) 最後です。語り手は驚愕し、怖気づいて邸から逃げだします。崩壊を目撃。

From that chamber, and from that mansion, I fled aghast. The storm was still abroad in all its wrath as I found myself crossing the old causeway. Suddenly there shot along the path a wild light, and I turned to see whence a gleam so unusual could have issued; for the vast house and its shadows were alone behind me. The radiance 5
was that of the full, setting, and blood-red moon which now shone vividly through that once barely discernible fissure, of which I have before spoken as extending from the roof of the building, in a zigzag direction, to the base. While I gazed, this fissure rapidly widened—there came a fierce breath of the whirlwind—the entire 10
orb of the satellite burst at once upon my sight—my brain reeled as I saw the mighty walls rushing asunder—there was a long tumultuous shouting sound like the voice of a thousand waters—and the deep and dank tarn at my feet closed sullenly and silently over the fragments of the 'House of Usher'. (p. 74) 15

Notes ●●●●●

1 **aghast**「仰天して」
1– **the storm was ... wrath**「嵐がまだどこでも激しく吹き荒れていた」この abroad は「どこもかしこも」という意味。
3 **causeway**「土手道、あぜ道」
4 **whence a gleam ... issued**「どこからそのような異常な光が発することなどあり得たか」仮定法過去完了です。if の部分は「たとえ可能だとしても」など。［英文法ガイド 9–IV–3］参照。
5 **were alone behind me**「私の背後にあるのは〜だけだった」
6 **setting**「没しつつある」cf. sunset「日没」
7 **once barely-discernible fissure**「かつてはやっと識別できた裂け目」
9 **to the base**「基部まで」extending にかかります。
10– **the entire orb ... my sight**「丸い月全体がすぐ私の視界に飛び込んできた」
12 **rushing asunder**「ものすごい勢いで裂ける、亀裂がどんどん広がる」
13 **a thousand waters**「無数の大波、洪水」
14 **deep and dank tarn at my feet**「足元の深く湿った沼」アッシャー家が裂け、亀裂の間から血色の満月が光り、最後に深い沼の中に轟音を上げて荒れ狂う波間に呑み込まれてゆく情景を描く、作者の華麗な詩的な文章に注目。

3. 『緋文字』

The Scarlet Letter
(1850)
by
Nathaniel Hawthorne

　ナサニエル・ホーソン Nathaniel Hawthorne (1804–64) は、アメリカ文学の黄金時代の代表的な小説家です。セイラムの古い清教徒の由緒ある家柄に生まれ、父を幼少時に亡くしています。先祖には魔女狩り裁判にかかわった判事がいて、早くから罪の意識に目覚め、作家として一生、罪の問題に取り組むことになりました。伯父の家に引き取られ、土地の大学に入学し、学生時代から創作を始め、人間の心の内奥を覗きこむような深刻な短編を書きました。ボストンの税関で働き、一時トランセンダリストの共同生活に参加しますが、脱退します。しかし、トランセンダリストの一人である、名家の女性と結婚。多少孤独から逃れ創作力を回復し、『緋文字』を発表して一躍文名が上がります。続けて『七破風の家』、『ブライスデール物語』を刊行。53 年には、大学での同級生が大統領になり、ホーソンはリヴァプールの領事になります。辞めた後、イタリアに 2 年間滞在し、『大理石の牧神』が生まれます。彼の小説は、人間の生活をそのままリアリズムで描くのではなく、現実と幻想が複雑に混じり合った有様を、シンボルやアレゴリーを用いて表現しています。

　17 世紀のボストンを舞台にする、姦通を扱った小説。美しいヘスターは、医師の夫が長期に留守している間に子供を産んだので、裁判にかけられ、服役後、衣服の胸にアダルタリー（姦通）の頭文字 A をつけて、曝し台で人目にさらされます。戻ってきた夫は、医師チリングワースと偽名を使い、姦通の相手は敬虔な牧師ディムズデールだと探り当てて執拗に責めます。牧師は、そのいじめで心身衰弱して行きます。ヘスターは天真爛漫な子供パールと周囲から好意を抱かれるようになります。彼女は、医師が実は夫であると牧師に教え、パールを連れて他の土地に逃亡しようと提案します。彼は、一時迷った後、最後に人々の前で罪を告白、ヘスターとパールに抱かれながら死んで行きます。2 つある映画は、共に原作の雰囲気から遠いようです。

Nathaniel Hawthorne

(1) ヘスターが胸にＡの文字をつけた服装で曝し台に立つ姿が描かれています。

 The door of the jail being flung open from within, there appeared, in the first place, like a black shadow emerging into the sunshine, the grim and grisly presence of the town-beadle, with a sword by his side and his staff of office in his hand. This personage prefigured and represented in his aspect the whole dismal severity of the　5 Puritanic code of law, which it was his business to administer in its final and closest application to the offender. Stretching forth the official staff in his left hand, he laid his right upon the shoulder of a young woman, whom he thus drew forward; until, on the threshold of the prison-door, she repelled him, by an action marked with　10 natural dignity and force of character, and stepped into the open air as if by her own free-will. →

Notes ●●●●
3 **grisly presence ... town-beadle**「裁判所の小役人の気味の悪い姿」
4 **staff of office**「官職を示す棒」
4– **prefigured and represented**「予め示し、かつ、表現した」目的語は the whole 以下。
6 **Puritanic code of law**「清教徒の法典」ここでは姦通罪。
6– **which it was his business ... offender**「その法典を、最終のもっとも厳密な適用段階において、罪人に対して、執行するのが彼の任務であった」一定期間刑務所に閉じ込めた後、解放するに先立ち、群衆の前で曝し台に立たせるのが「最終段階の罰」。
8 **his right** 次に省略されているのは hand です。
10 **repelled him**「追い払った」法律上は、罪人にそんなことは出来ないのですが、彼女の場合は、威厳があって、役人は思わず遠慮してしまったのです。

The Scarlet Letter

→ She bore in her arms a child, a baby of some three months old, who winked and turned aside its little face from the too vivid light of day; because its existence, heretofore, had brought it acquainted only with the grey twilight of a dungeon, or other darksome apartment of the prison.

When the young woman—the mother of this child—stood fully revealed before the crowd, it seemed to be her first impulse to clasp the infant closely to her bosom; not so much by an impulse of motherly affection, as that she might thereby conceal a certain token, which was wrought or fastened into her dress. In a moment, however, wisely judging that one token of her shame would but poorly serve to hide another, she took the baby on her arm, and, with a burning blush, and yet a haughty smile, and a glance that would not be abashed, looked around at her townspeople and neighbours. On the breast of her gown, in fine red cloth, surrounded with an elaborate embroidery and fantastic flourishes of gold thread, appeared the letter A. (Ch. 2, pp. 49–50)

*N*otes ●●●●

14– **its existence ... dungeon**「赤ん坊の生活はこれまで地下牢の暗い薄明りにしか接していなかった」
15 **brought it acquainted only with ~**「赤ん坊に経験させたのは〜だけだった」
19– **not so much ... as that ~**「... というよりは〜という目的で」
20 **thereby**「それによって」胸に赤ん坊を抱きしめれば、胸の印を群集の目から隠せるわけです。
21 **wrought or fastened**「縫い込んであったか、しっかり止めてあったか」
22– **one token ... another**「恥の一つの印はもう一方の印を隠すのに不十分にしか役立たぬ」胸の烙印も赤ん坊も姦通の証拠ですから。
25 **would not be abashed**「たじろがされるものか」「負けるものか」
27 **flourishes of gold thread**「金糸を風変わりに刺繍した飾り」

75

Nathaniel Hawthorne

(2) 最後の場面。ディムズデール牧師が罪を告白します。

　With a convulsive motion, he tore away the ministerial band from before his breast. It was revealed! But it were irreverent to describe that revelation. For an instant, the gaze of the horror-stricken multitude was concentrated on the ghastly miracle; while the minister stood, with a flush of triumph in his face, as one who, in the crisis of acutest pain, had won a victory. Then, down he sank upon the scaffold! Hester partly raised him, and supported his head against her bosom. Old Roger Chillingworth knelt down beside him, with a blank, dull countenance, out of which the life seemed to have departed. →

*N*otes ●●●●●

1　**ministerial band**「牧師が首につける広襟」胸まで垂れさがっているので、from before「胸の前から」はぎ取るのです。
2　**It was revealed**「それは現れた」it はヘスター胸の A と同じ烙印で、牧師は自分の胸にもその印があると群衆に告白したのです。
2-　**It were irreverent ... revelation**「その現れを描写するのは、不敬でありましょう」この were は古風な英語で今なら would be を使います。仮定法で、「もし描写したら」という感じ。［英文法ガイド 9-IV-3］参照。
4　**ghastly miracle**「恐るべき奇跡」その烙印があることです。
6　**down he sank**「くずれるように倒れた」これは強調のために通常の sank down という語順と違います。

→ "Thou hast escaped me!" he repeated more than once. "Thou hast escaped me!"

"My God forgive thee!" said the minister. "Thou, too, hast deeply sinned!"

He withdrew his dying eyes from the old man, and fixed them on the woman and the child.

"My little Pearl," said he, feebly and there was a sweet and gentle smile over his face, as of a spirit sinking into deep repose; nay, now that the burden was removed, it seemed almost as if he would be sportive with the child—"dear little Pearl, wilt thou kiss me now? Thou wouldst not, yonder, in the forest! But now thou wilt?" (Ch. 23, pp. 221–22)

Notes ●●●●●

13 **My God forgive thee!**　祈願文です。[英文法ガイド 9–IV–6] 参照。
18 **as of ... repose**　「深い安息へと沈んでゆく人のらしい（優しい微笑）」
19 **nay** = no. すぐ前で死んで行く人らしい、と述べたのを否定しています。そうではなく、パール相手に戯れるような明るい気分になっていた、と訂正しています。
    now that the burden was removed　告白によって心の重荷が除かれた、というのです。
    it seemed almost as if ~　「ほとんど~であるかのように思えた」
20– **wilt thou kiss me**　今の英語なら will you kiss me です。
21 **Thou wouldst not**　ここも今なら You would not です。
    yonder, in the forest　あっちの方で、つまり、森では、ということ。以前森で親子三人で会い、ヘスターが皆で逃亡しようと提案したのですが、その時パールは彼にキスしようとしなかったのです。

4.『白鯨』

Moby-Dick; or, The Whale
(1851)
by
Herman Melvill

　ハーマン・メルヴィル Herman Melvill (1819–91) はニューヨークの富裕な貿易商の一家に生まれました。少年時代は恵まれていましたが、父の破産と死のため高等教育を受けることができなくなり、19歳で船員となります。「捕鯨船こそ、私にとってのイエール大学でありハーヴァード大学であった」とは作中人物イシュメイルの言葉ですが、メルヴィル本人の言葉としてもたびたび引用されて有名になりました。

　船に乗り組んだ経験を生かして書いた『タイピー』(1846)『オムー』(1847) などの南海冒険小説で人気を博しますが、ホーソンの影響を受けて取り組んだ『白鯨』は、ごく一部の人々にしか認められませんでした。中間章での脱線、さまざまに変化する文体など、当時の一般読者の常識を超えた小説だったためでしょう。晩年は一税関吏として世間から忘れられた存在のまま世を去りますが、生誕百年を契機に再評価され、今日『白鯨』は世界文学を代表する作品の一つです。モームによる世界の十大小説にもアメリカから唯一選ばれています。

　『白鯨』の語り手イシュメイルは、捕鯨船ピークオド号に乗って海に出ます。あらゆる人種の船員が乗り組むこの船は、世界の縮図のようです。船長エイハブは噂に包まれた謎の人物で、自分の片脚を奪った巨大な白鯨モビー・ディックへの復讐を誓い、乗組員を巻き込んで白鯨を追います。ついに姿を現した白鯨と三日にわたる死闘の末、奇跡的に生き残るのはイシュメイル一人だけという運命が待ち受けていたのです。

　三回目の映画化であるジョン・ヒューストン監督の 1956 年版は、海洋小説の傑作としての魅力を生かして上手にまとめられ、格調が高く、迫力があります。が、原作はただの海洋冒険小説ではありません。イシュメイル、エイハブなどの旧約聖書に由来する名前、聖書の引用、シェイクスピアのような台詞の数々、哲学的な観念なども豊富で、さまざまの読み方ができる、スケールの大きな一編なのです。

　ここでは冒頭と、甲板でのエイハブ船長のシーン、どちらも有名な一節を読んでみましょう。

Moby-Dick; or, The Whale

(1) 語り手イシュメイルが物語を始める冒頭の一節です。

　　Call me Ishmael. Some years ago—never mind how long precisely—having little or no money in my purse, and nothing particular to interest me on shore, I thought I would sail about a little and see the watery part of the world. It is a way I have of driving off the spleen and regulating the circulation. Whenever I find myself growing grim about the mouth; whenever it is a damp, drizzly November in my soul; whenever I find myself involuntarily pausing before coffin warehouses, and bringing up the rear of every funeral I meet; and especially whenever my hypos get such an upper hand of me, that it requires a strong moral principle to prevent me from deliberately stepping into the street, and methodically knocking people's hats off—then, I account it high time to get to sea as soon as I can. This is my substitute for pistol and ball. (Ch. 1, p. 3)

*N*otes ●●●●

1　**Call me Ishmael**　有名なセンテンス、もちろん命令文です。Ishmael「イシュメイル」は語り手をつとめる青年の名で、「追放者」の意味があります。自己紹介ですが、このわずか三語の単純な一文については、いろいろ議論されてきました。これまで十以上ある邦訳でも訳し方はそれぞれ異なっていて、翻訳は訳者の解釈が問われるものだということの、良い一例です。

2-　**having ... on shore**　理由を表わす分詞構文。[英文法ガイド 5-I-1] 参照。

2　**nothing**　上の having の目的語です。

3　**on shore**　ここでは海に対して「陸地で」。

4　**the watery part of the world**「水の世界」すなわち海のこと。
　　a way I have of　I have は挿入句で a way of と続きます。

5　**circulation**「血行」

5-　**growing grim about the mouth**「口の辺りに不快感を覚えるようになる」

8　**bringing up the rear**「後ろからついて行く」bring up the rear = follow behind.

9　**my hypos ... me**「憂鬱病が私を支配する」get the upper hand of = defeat.

12　**then, I account it high time to get to sea**　high time とは「潮時、とっくに〜すべき時」の意味です。Whenever で始まる文中で具体例を次々と挙げていき、ここでまとめて「そういう時には〜」と展開しています。

13　**substitute**「代替品」何の代わりにどうするというのか、確認してください。
　　ball「弾丸」

Herman Melvill

(2) エイハブ船長が乗組員たちを前にして船の目的を語る場面です。

"What do ye do when ye see a whale, men?"
"Sing out for him!" was the impulsive rejoinder from a score of clubbed voices.
"Good!" cried Ahab, with a wild approval in his tones; observing the hearty animation into which his unexpected question had so magnetically thrown them.
"And what do ye next, men?"
"Lower away, and after him!"
"And what tune is it ye pull to, men?"
"A dead whale or a stove boat!"
More and more strangely and fiercely glad and approving, grew the countenance of the old man at every shout; while the mariners began to gaze curiously at each other, as if marvelling how it was that they themselves became so excited at such seemingly purposeless questions. (Ch. 36, p. 175)

Notes ●●●●

1 **ye** 二人称単数 thou の複数形。「おまえたち、なんじら」
2 **sing out**「大声を上げる、叫ぶ」／ 2- **a score of clubbed voices** score は 20、clubbed は「統一された、集まっている」
4 **Ahab**「エイハブ」ピークオド号船長。白鯨への復讐の念に燃えています。
5 **hearty animation**「元気あふれる様子、大いに活気を帯びた様子」
into which 前置詞＋関係代名詞。[英文法ガイド 8-I-3] 参照。
6 **magnetically**「磁石で引き寄せるように」
8 **Lower away**「ボートを下ろす」海事用語です。
and after him「そして彼を追います」動詞などを省略した簡潔な表現。
9 **what tune is it ye pull to**「どういう歌に合わせて漕ぐのか？」Cf. Alice danced to music.「アリスは音楽に合わせて踊った」pull「（ボートなどを）漕ぐ」
10 **A dead whale or a stove boat**「鯨を殺すか、こちらのボートに穴をあけられるか」こんな歌詞の歌を歌いながら漕いだのでしょうか。stove は stave の過去分詞。鯨によって船体に穴をあけられれば船は沈没。当時の捕鯨はこのようなものでした。／ 11 **approving**「大賛成で、よしよしというように」
12 **old man** エイハブ船長の言い換えですね。／ 13- **how it was that ~**「というのはいったいどういうわけなのか」it は that 以下を指します。

Moby-Dick; or, The Whale

(3) エイハブ船長の有名な台詞です。

　　. . . Then tossing both arms, with measureless imprecations he shouted out: "Aye, aye! and I'll chase him round Good Hope, and round the Horn, and round the Norway Maelstrom, and round perdition's flames before I give him up. And this is what ye have shipped for, men! to chase that white whale on both sides of land, and over all sides of earth, till he spouts black blood and rolls fin out. What say ye, men, will ye splice hands on it, now? I think ye do look brave."

　"Aye, aye!" shouted the harpooneers and seamen, running closer to the excited old man: "A sharp eye for the White Whale; a sharp lance for Moby Dick!" (Ch. 36, p. 177)

Notes ●●●●●

1　**with measureless imprecations**「計り知れぬ恨みをこめて」
2　**Aye, aye!**　aye = yes.
　him　Moby Dick を指します。
　Good Hope = the Cape of Good Hope.「喜望峰」アフリカ南端の岬。
3　**the Horn** = Cape Horn.「ホーン岬」南米大陸最南端の岬。悪天候で有名な航海の難所。
　Norway Maelstrom「ノルウェーのメールストローム」「モスケンの大渦巻」ともいいます。船が吸い込まれると信じられていた危険な渦巻きで、Poe にもこれを題材とする短編があります。
4　**perdition's flames**「地獄の火」つまり地獄まで追いかける、というのです。
4–　**what ye have shipped for**「なんじらが乗船した目的」
6–　**rolls fin out**「尾びれを平たくする」横倒しになるのは死んだ証拠です。
7　**splice hands on ~**「~に同意する」そのことについて皆で手を組む、が文字通り。
7–　**ye do look brave**　do は強調。
11　**lance**「(鯨を突く)もり、やす」

5.『若草物語』

Little Women
(1868)
by
Louisa May Alcott

　ルイザ・メイ・オルコット Louisa May Alcott (1832–88) はペンシルヴェニア州に生まれ、少女時代をボストンで過ごしました。父のブロンソンは理想家肌の教育者で、あまり生活力があるとは言えない人でした。小さい時から書くことを好み、家計を助ける手段としてスリラー、ゴシック、妖精物語などを書いていたオルコットが、少女向きの物語をという出版社からの依頼を受けて 35 歳で書き始めたのが、この『若草物語』です。これによってオルコットは、アメリカの家庭小説の礎を築いた作家として有名になりました。好評のため続編も次々に書かれています。

　原題は Little Women で、日本では『小婦人』『四人姉妹』『四人の少女』などと訳されてきました。『若草物語』というタイトルは、1934 年の矢田津世子・水谷まさるによる訳書からで、この前年に輸入されたアメリカ映画の日本版の監修をした吉屋信子が映画のタイトルとして選んだ『若草物語』という訳語が、その後定着したものです。

　舞台はニューイングランド、父が南北戦争の従軍牧師として留守の間、母を中心に家を守るマーチ家の四人姉妹の物語です。作家としてのオルコットの腕前が光る冒頭部分を引用しますが、その少しあとに戦場の父から届いた手紙を母が 4 人の娘に読み聞かせる場面があり、その文中で父が娘たちのことを my little women と呼んでいます。自分が留守の間も各々の務めを果たし、立派な女性として頑張ってほしい、という、父から娘たちへの望み——ここで一編の題名の意味も分かります。小説全体として家庭や結婚に大きな価値を置く伝統的な女性観があるのは明らかですが、少女小説につきものの感傷を排した、飾り気のない文体が画期的で、ボーヴォワールなど、これまで多くの女性を力づけてきました。賢く愛情深いマーチ夫人と、それぞれ長所も短所もある四人姉妹の生き生きした人物像、そして信頼と温かさのあふれる家庭生活が魅力的です。これまで何度も映画化され、愛されてきましたが、中でも最新の 1993 年版は格調の高い名作です。

Little Women

(1) クリスマスイブの夕方、母の帰宅を待つ4人姉妹の光景が小説の冒頭です。

"Christmas won't be Christmas without any presents," grumbled Jo, lying on the rug.

"It's so dreadful to be poor!" sighed Meg, looking down at her old dress.

"I don't think it's fair for some girls to have lots of pretty things, and other girls nothing at all," added little Amy, with an injured sniff.

"We've got father and mother, and each other, anyhow," said Beth, contentedly, from her corner.

The four young faces on which the firelight shone brightened at the cheerful words, but darkened again as Jo said sadly,—

"We haven't got father, and shall not have him for a long time." She didn't say "perhaps never," but each silently added it, thinking of father far away, where the fighting was. →

*N*otes ●●●●

1 **without**「～がなければ」
2 **Jo** マーチ家の次女で15歳のジョー。活発で自立心が強く、作家志望の女の子という設定で、作者のオルコット自身がモデルと言われます。
  lying on the rug rugは床の一部や炉の前に敷く敷物のこと。敷物に寝そべって言った、という状況描写から、読者はいろいろなことがわかるのでは？短い中にも四人それぞれの性格が表れた発言と描写がこの後にも続きます。たちまちのうちに読者を物語の世界に引きこむ見事な冒頭です。
3 **Meg**「メグ」16歳のメグ。美人でおしゃれ。
5 **for some girls to ~** 不定詞の意味上の主語。[英文法ガイド3-III] 参照。
6 **Amy**「エイミー」12歳の末っ子。絵を描くのが上手。
8 **Beth**「ベス」13歳の三女。病弱ですが忍耐強く、音楽好きの、心優しい女の子。
8 **from her corner** herに注意しましょう。「彼女の（いつもの）隅」
11 **haven't got** = don't have. 現在完了の意味ではありません。この形、会話ではよく使われます。

Louisa May Alcott

→ Nobody spoke for a minute; then Meg said in an altered tone,—

"You know the reason mother proposed not having any presents this Christmas, was because it's going to be a hard winter for every one; and she thinks we ought not to spend money for pleasure, when our men are suffering so in the army. We can't do much, but we can make our little sacrifices, and ought to do it gladly. But I am afraid I don't;" and Meg shook her head, as she thought regretfully of all the pretty things she wanted.

"But I don't think the little we should spend would do any good. We've each got a dollar, and the army wouldn't be much helped by our giving that. I agree not to expect anything from mother or you, but I do want to buy Undine and Sintram for myself; I've wanted it *so* long," said Jo, who was a bookworm.

"I planned to spend mine in new music," said Beth, with a little sigh, which no one heard but the hearth-brush and kettle-holder.

"I shall get a nice box of Faber's drawing pencils; I really need them," said Amy, decidedly. (Ch. 1, p. 1)

*N*otes ••••

- 15 **the reason mother ...**　that または why が省略されています。これも会話ではよくある形。
- 25 **Undine and Sintram**　ドイツロマン派の作家フケー Friedrich de la Motte Fouque (1777–1843) の書いた物語。代表作『ウンディーネ』(1811) は水の精と騎士の恋物語、『ジントラムの道連れ』(1814) も騎士物語で、ともに英訳されて親しまれました。両方を一冊にして出された書名を、ここではジョーが短縮して言っているものと思われます。
- 26 **bookworm**　いわゆる「本の虫」、つまり本好き、読書好きのことです。
- 27 **music**「楽譜」
- 28 **but the hearth-brush and kettle-holder**「暖炉用の刷毛と鍋つかみの他には」but = except.
- 29 **Faber**「ファーバー」鉛筆会社として 1761 年創立のドイツの文具・画材メーカーの名。
- 30 **decidedly**「きっぱりと」

Little Women

(2) 母親のマーチ夫人が帰って来ます。

"Glad to find you so merry, my girls," said a cheery voice at the door, and actors and audience turned to welcome a stout, motherly lady, with a "can-I-help-you" look about her which was truly delightful. She wasn't a particularly handsome person, but mothers are always lovely to their children, and the girls thought the gray cloak and unfashionable bonnet covered the most splendid woman in the world.

"Well, dearies, how have you got on to-day? There was so much to do, getting the boxes ready to go to-morrow, that I didn't come home to dinner. Has any one called, Beth? How is your cold, Meg? Jo, you look tired to death. Come and kiss me, baby."

While making these maternal inquiries Mrs. March got her wet things off, her hot slippers on, and sitting down in the easy-chair, drew Amy to her lap, preparing to enjoy the happiest hour of her busy day. The girls flew about, trying to make things comfortable, each in her own way. (Ch. 1, p. 7)

Notes •••••

1 **Glad to find you so merry, my girls.** 文頭の I'm が省略されています。merry は補語。[英文法ガイド 1–II] 参照。girls は daughters の意味。
2 **actors and audience** 四人は母の帰りを待つ間、交替で劇の人物を演じて楽しんでいたのです。／3 **"can-I-help-you" look** 常に "Can I help you?" と訊ねているかのような雰囲気の女性を思い浮かべてください。
4 **handsome** 男性の「ハンサム」だけではなく、女性の場合には、りりしくりっとした顔立ち、また中年以降の女性の美しさに使います。
4– **mothers are always lovely to their children** 現在形にしているのは一般論だからですね。
8 **dearies** deary は主に女性が用いる呼びかけ。
how have you got on cf. How are you getting on?「ごきげんいかがですか?」
10 **dinner**「正餐」一日のうちの主要な食事のことで、通例は夕食ですが、この場合のようにお昼に dinner をとれば、夕食が supper になります。
Has any one called この call は、現在なら電話ですが、この時代では「訪問する」です。／11 **Come and kiss me, baby** 末っ子 Amy への呼びかけです。
15 **flew about**「飛び回った」

6.『ワシントン・スクエア（女相続人）』

Washington Square
(1880)
by
Henry James

　ヘンリー・ジェイムズ Henry James (1843–1916) はニューヨークに生まれ、晩年にイギリスに帰化した小説家で、近代心理小説の祖と言われます。視点となる人物を用いて、意識や心理を通して物語を進めるという、それ以前の小説にない方法で独特の世界を築きました。父親の考えでヨーロッパ滞在が多く、ハーバード大学に入学しましたが、退学して創作活動を始めました。初期には『ロデリック・ハドソン』、『デイジー・ミラー』など国際状況をテーマとする小説が多く、集大成は『ある婦人の肖像』です。劇作などを試みた中期を経て、円熟期の三大長編『鳩の翼』、『使者たち』、『黄金の杯』を完成します。

　ジェイムズの作品は複雑な構造と文体のために難解なことで知られますが、初期に書かれたこの『ワシントン・スクエア』(1880) は、比較的読みやすいものの一つです。

　主人公のキャサリンは、容姿には恵まれないものの素直で正直な娘で、父親のスローパー博士を心から愛し、尊敬しています。ハンサムな青年モリス・タウンゼンドに出会って恋に落ちますが、スローパー博士はモリスを財産目当ての求婚者と信じて疑わず、もし自分の同意を得ない相手と結婚すれば財産は譲らないとキャサリンに言い渡します。実は博士の過去には、大いに将来を期待していた第一子の長男をわずか三歳で、キャサリンの誕生直後には最愛の妻をも亡くしたため、理想の女性であった亡き妻との比較で平凡な娘キャサリンに失望してきたという経緯があります。一方、お洒落で社交上手な青年モリス、スローパー博士の妹でキャサリンの母親代わりをつとめるペニマン夫人——この四人の主要な登場人物が生き生きと描き分けられている点にも注目してください。

　映画化された『女相続人』は映画史に残る名作ですが原作とは異なる展開もあり、原作と映画との比較も大変興味深いと思います。ここに引用した原文は、ジェイムズならではの細やかな文章で博士とキャサリンについて説明している箇所です。文学の醍醐味を十分に味わってください。

Washington Square

(1) 第一章でスローパー博士のこれまでが説明されています。

　. . . Even at the age of twenty-seven Austin Sloper had made his mark sufficiently to mitigate the anomaly of his having been chosen among a dozen suitors by a young woman of high fashion, who had ten thousand dollars of income and the most charming eyes in the island of Manhattan. These eyes, and some of their accompaniments, were for about five years a source of extreme satisfaction to the young physician, who was both a devoted and a very happy husband.

　The fact of his having married a rich woman made no difference in the line he had traced for himself, and he cultivated his profession with as definite a purpose as if he still had no other resources than his fraction of the modest patrimony which, on his father's death, he had shared with his brothers and sisters. (Ch. 1, p. 28)

*N*otes ●●●●

2　**mark**　make one's mark「名をあげる、成功する」ここでは時制が過去完了であることを見逃さないように。／**mitigate**「やわらげる、緩和する」／**anomaly**　変則的なこと。次の of は同格で「～という」。何が、なぜ変則的なのか、ここでの内容を考えてみること。

3　**dozen**　1 ダースは 12 ですが、正確に 12 とは限らず、「1 ダース前後」を示すこともよくあります。
　a young woman of high fashion　a man (woman) of fashion という表現に注意。「若い上流婦人」

4　**income**「収入、所得」ここでは財産から得られるものを指します。

5　**Manhattan**「マンハッタン」言うまでもなく、ニューヨーク市の中枢を成す島。

6　**accompaniments**「付随物」ですが、美しい目とその付随物のいくつか、とは？

7　**the young physician**「若い医師」とは？ もちろんスローパー博士のこと。英語ではこのように、同一の語の繰り返しを避けて言いかえることがよくあるので注意。／**devoted**「熱愛している」

10　**the line he ... for himself**「彼がとってきた方針」
　cultivated his profession「仕事である医学に専念した」

11　**resources**「資産、財産」

12　**modest**　いろいろの意味がありますが、前に fraction of とあり、また財産について述べている文だということを考慮して「（数量が）あまり多くない」の意味だとわかれば正解です。常に文脈を大事に。[英文法ガイド 12] 参照。

Henry James

(2) キャサリン誕生前後のスローパー博士の心理が語られています。

  ... His first child, a little boy of extraordinary promise, as the Doctor, who was not addicted to easy enthusiasms, firmly believed, died at three years of age, in spite of everything that the mother's tenderness and the father's science could invent to save him. Two years later Mrs. Sloper gave birth to a second infant—an infant of a sex which rendered the poor child, to the Doctor's sense, an inadequate substitute for his lamented first-born, of whom he had promised himself to make an admirable man. The little girl was a disappointment; but this was not the worst. A week after her birth the young mother, who, as the phrase is, had been doing well, suddenly betrayed alarming symptoms, and before another week had elapsed Austin Sloper was a widower. (Ch. 1, p. 29)

*N*otes ●●●●

1 **promise**「約束」の意味なら誰でも知っていますが、ここも前後を考えて辞書を引き直し、「前途、将来の有望さ、見込み」という、ぴったりの日本語を探し当ててほしいものです。

2 **was not addicted ... enthusiasm**「簡単に感激する癖がない」

5– **an infant of a sex ~**「～となるような性別の赤ちゃん」つまりここでは「女の赤ちゃん」のことです。

7 **inadequate substitute**「物足りない代用」

7– **of whom ... admirable man**「立派な男にしてみせると博士自身が誓った」Cf. Make a good singer of my son.「息子を良い歌手に育ててください」

10 **as the phrase is**「そういう言い方をよくするのですが」という意味合いです。どこについて言っているのでしょうか？
  had been doing well do well は「健康に、元気で」の意味。ここではお産なので、「産後の経過が順調」という表現に当たります。had been となっているのはどうしてでしょうか？ 時制には常に注意をはらいましょう。

11 **betrayed alarming symptoms**「危険な兆候をみせた」

(3) さて、主人公のキャサリンはどんな娘でしょうか。

... 'When Catherine is about seventeen,' he said to himself, 'Lavinia will try and persuade her that some young man with a moustache is in love with her. It will be quite untrue; no young man, with a moustache or without, will ever be in love with Catherine. But Lavinia will take it up, and talk to her about it; perhaps even, if her taste for clandestine operations doesn't prevail with her, she will talk to me about it. Catherine won't see it, and won't believe it, fortunately for her peace of mind; poor Catherine isn't romantic.'

She was a healthy, well-grown child, without a trace of her mother's beauty. She was not ugly; she had simply a plain, dull, gentle countenance. The most that had ever been said for her was that she had a 'nice' face, and, though she was an heiress, no one had ever thought of regarding her as a belle. Her father's opinion of her moral purity was abundantly justified; she was excellently, imperturbably good; affectionate, docile, obedient, and much addicted to speaking the truth. (Ch. 2, pp. 33–34)

Notes ●●●●

2 **Lavinia** Mrs. Penniman のファーストネーム。ここは博士が妹と娘をどう見ているかが表れている一節です。
  try and persuade to に置き換えればよい and です。
5 **take it up**「そういう考えを抱く」
6 **if her taste ... with her**「ラヴィニアの秘密の作戦趣味が娘を説き伏せなければ」prevail with「説き伏せる」Cf. I tried but could not prevail with him. 彼を説き伏せようとしたが、だめだった。
10 **plain** 女性の容貌についてこの形容詞を用いた場合、婉曲に「美しくない、不器量な」と言っていることになります。
12 **'nice'**「感じの良い」ですが、引用符に注意。周囲の人がキャサリンの器量を褒める言葉に困って使った形容を引用しているのです。
  heiress「女相続人」相当な財産を相続する見込みのある場合に限って使われます。
13 **belle**「美人」

7.『ハックルベリー・フィンの冒険』

Adventures of Huckleberry Finn
(1885)
by
Mark Twain

　マーク・トウェイン Mark Twain (1835–1910) は、ミズーリ州フロリダの開拓者の家に生まれました。本名はサミュエル・ラングホーン・クレメンズ (Samuel Langhorne Clemens) といいます。ミシシッピー河畔の小さい町ハンニバルで少年時代を過ごしました。12歳の時に父を亡くし、学校をやめて植字工見習いになり、兄の経営する新聞に記事を書いたりもしました。南北戦争前にはミシシッピー川の蒸気船の水先案内人として働きます。ペンネームの「マーク・トウェイン」は、船の航行に必要な「水深2ひろ」のかけ声です。その後西部で新聞通信員となって、「ジム・スマイリーと飛び蛙」や『赤毛布外遊記』などの作品によって有名作家となりました。東部の富豪の娘オリヴィアと結婚、コネティカット州ハートフォードに住みますが、娘二人と妻に先立たれるという不幸にあい、晩年には厭世的な作風になりました。興味深い自伝も残しています。

　さて、代表作の『トム・ソーヤーの冒険』(1876) とその続編『ハックルベリー・フィンの冒険』は、どちらも冒険小説に特有のエピソード形式で書かれ、大人中心の文明社会への批判、子供の世界と自然への賛美という柱を持つ点が共通です。トムとハックは友達で、両作品に登場します。ただし大きな違いとして、『トム・ソーヤーの冒険』が三人称で書かれているのに対し、『ハックルベリー・フィンの冒険』はハック自身が口語で語る一人称形式であるため臨場感があります。また、『トム・ソーヤーの冒険』では子供時代の賛美が色濃く出ているのに対し、この作品の主人公ハックは浮浪児で、逃亡奴隷のジムと共に筏でミシシッピー川を下りながら大人の世界の醜さや愚かさを体験し、成長するストーリーです。ヘミングウェイが「すべての現代アメリカ文学は『ハック・フィン』という一冊の本に源を発している」と述べたことはよく知られていますが、出版当時は禁書処分にした図書館もあったほど問題の書でした。

　映画『ハックフィンの大冒険』ではイライジャ・ウッドのハックがやや可愛らしすぎる印象ですが、良心と心情の間で苦しみ悩む姿がよく描かれています。

Adventures of Huckleberry Finn

(1) 小説の冒頭、ハックが語り始めます。

 You don't know about me without you have read a book by the name of *The Adventures of Tom Sawyer*, but that ain't no matter. That book was made by Mr. Mark Twain, and he told the truth, mainly. There was things which he stretched, but mainly he told the truth. That is nothing. I never seen anybody but lied, one time or another, without it was Aunt Polly, or the widow, or maybe Mary. Aunt Polly—Tom's Aunt Polly, she is—and Mary, and the Widow Douglas, is all told about in that book—which is mostly a true book; with some stretchers, as I said before. →

*N*otes ●●●●●

1 **You don't know about me ...** ハックが語り手として、読者にむかって話し始めます。
 without = unless. この用法は俗語的です。
2 ***The Adventures of Tom Sawyer*** 『トム・ソーヤーの冒険』トムとハックがこの前作で、洞窟に隠されていた金貨を発見して大金持ちになったことは、次の段落に書かれています。
4 **There was** 文法上で正しくは were です。他にも正しくない箇所がいくつもあるのですが、意味は理解できますし、ハックらしさがよく出ていますね。
 stretched 「誇張した」
5 **anybody but lied** = anybody that has not lied. 「嘘をついたことがない人」but は否定を伴う関係代名詞。Cf. There is no rule but has some exceptions. 「例外のない規則はない」
6 **Aunt Polly** 「ポリー伯母さん」両親を亡くしたトムを育ててくれています。
 the widow = Widow Douglas. 「(ダグラス)未亡人」ハックの養育者。
 Mary 「メアリ」トムのいとこ。年上で優しい人です。
8 **is all told about** 「皆語られている」その本に登場し、どういう人か述べられている、というのです。
9 **some stretchers** 「いくらかの誇張」

Mark Twain

→ Now the way that the book winds up, is this: Tom and me found the money that the robbers hid in the cave, and it made us rich. We got six thousand dollars apiece—all gold. It was an awful sight of money when it was piled up. Well, Judge Thatcher, he took it and put it out at interest, and it fetched us a dollar a day apiece, all the year round—more than a body could tell what to do with. The Widow Douglas, she took me for her son, and allowed she would sivilize me; but it was rough living in the house all the time, considering how dismal regular and decent the widow was in all her ways; and so when I couldn't stand it no longer, I lit out. I got into my old rags, and my sugar-hogshead again, and was free and satisfied. But Tom Sawyer, he hunted me up and said he was going to start a band of robbers, and I might join if I would go back to the widow and be respectable. So I went back. (Ch. 1, p. 49)

*N*otes ●●●●

- 10 **winds up**「結局～になる、～ということで終わる」
- 13 **Judge Thatcher**「サッチャー判事」その娘のベッキーはトムの憧れの女の子。
- 14 **put it out at interest**「利子つきで貸した」
- 16 **allowed**（アメリカ方言）「言った」
- 17 **sivilize** civilize と書くべきところ、ハックがつづりを間違えています。
  It was rough living「暮らすのはきつかった」It は動名詞の living 以下を指します。
- 18– **how dismal ... her ways**「ダグラスさんが、あらゆる面でどんなに気がめいるほど規則正しく健全であるか」ハックは堅苦しさや束縛が大嫌いです。
- 19 **couldn't stand it no longer** 二重否定の形ですが、「もう我慢できなくなった」の意ですから否定語は一つ余計です。強く否定したい気持ちが働いて、思わず否定語を二回使ってしまったのです。
  lit out「逃亡した」現在形は light out。
- 20 **sugar-hogshead** 浮浪児のハックは、「（砂糖の入っていた）大樽、砂糖の空き樽」を住みかにしていたのです。いつも家の中にいるのは辛い、と述べていた理由もわかりますね。
- 21 **hunted me up**「おれを捜し当てた」
- 23 **be respectable**「上品な生活をする」

Adventures of Huckleberry Finn

(2) 逃亡奴隷は告発すべきだという社会の掟とジムへの友情との間でハックが悩む場面です。

I felt good and all washed clean of sin for the first time I had ever felt so in my life, and I knowed I could pray now. But I didn't do it straight off, but laid the paper down and set there thinking—thinking how good it was all this happened so, and how near I come to being lost and going to hell. And went on thinking. And got to thinking over our trip down the river; and I see Jim before me, all the time, in the day, and in the night-time, sometimes moonlight, sometimes storms, and we a floating along, talking, and singing, and laughing. But somehow I couldn't seem to strike no places to harden me against him, but only the other kind. →

*N*otes ●●●●●

1 **I felt good** ハックは、社会的道徳に従うことを要求する良心と、自分の自然な反応である「心」との板挟みになって迷った末に逃亡奴隷ジムの居場所を教える手紙を書きました。それで悩みから解放された気持ちになったのです。
2 **knowed** knew と言うべきところ。このような文法やつづりの間違いはハックにとって日常茶飯事です。
3 **straight off**「即座に」
  the paper「例の紙」自分で書いた告発の手紙です。
4 **how good ... happened so** it は all this happened so という名詞節を指します。all の前に接続詞 that があるのが普通です。
6 **Jim** 逃亡奴隷のジム。ミス・ワトソンによって売られることを聞いて逃げ出してきました。
8 **we** ジムと二人だったことを回想すると「おれたち」という言葉が自然に出てきたのです。
  a floating この a は本来不要で、入れるのは俗語の用法です。Cf. go a hunting = go hunting.「狩猟に行く」
9 **couldn't seem to strike no places to harden me against him**「ジムのことを悪く思いたくなるようなことはないようで」ここも否定語が一つ余計に入った、通常の否定の意味。

Mark Twain

→ I'd see him standing my watch on top of his'n, stead of calling me, so I could go on sleeping; and see him how glad he was when I come back out of the fog; and when I come to him again in the swamp, up there where the feud was; and such-like times; and would always call me honey, and pet me, and do everything he could think of for me, and how good he always was; and at last I struck the time I saved him by telling the men we had small-pox aboard, and he was so grateful, and said I was the best friend old Jim ever had in the world, and the *only* one he's got now; and then I happened to look around, and see that paper.

It was a close place. I took it up, and held it in my hand. I was a trembling, because I'd got to decide, forever, betwixt two things, and I knowed it. I studied a minute, sort of holding my breath, and then says to myself:

'All right, then, I'll *go* to hell'—and tore it up.

(Ch. 31, pp. 282–83)

*N*otes ●●●●

- 11 **standing my watch ... his'n**「ジム自身の番の見張りをやったのに加えて、おれの番の見張りまでやってくれた」交替で見張り番をすることになっていたのです。his'n = his.「自分の見張り番」方言、俗語です。
  stead of = instead of.
- 16 **struck the time**「時のことが頭に浮かんだ」
- 17 **small-pox aboard**「天然痘患者が筏に乗っている」そう嘘をついたのです。
- 22 **betwixt** アメリカ南部の方言で between。
- 23 **studied**「どうすべきか検討した」
  sort of = kind of.「ちょっと」表現を和らげるために、副詞的に用います。
- 25 **All right, then, I'll *go* to hell** 逃亡奴隷告発の手紙を出さずにジムへの友情を優先したいという自分の心に従うには、大げさではなくこれだけの決断が必要だったのです。奴隷制度は神も認めた神聖不可侵の制度であり、逃亡奴隷を助けることは犯罪だ、と教えられて育った少年であることが良くわかる一節です。

8.『シスター・キャリー（黄昏）』

Sister Carrie
(1900)
by
Theodore Dreiser

　セオドア・ドライサー Theodore Dreiser (1871-1945) はカトリック系ドイツ移民の子としてインディアナ州に生まれ、貧困の中で育ちます。新聞記者や編集者の仕事をしながら大都市の現実を知るとともに、ハーバート・スペンサーの社会進化論等を読んで影響を受け、処女作『シスター・キャリー』を書き上げますが、この本の出版をめぐってはトラブル続出でした。1925年発表の大作『アメリカの悲劇』はアメリカ自然主義の頂点とされる一編で、出版後一年でベストセラーになりました。同時代の批評家に高く評価され、若い作家たちにも大きな影響を与えましたが、文体が武骨で統一がないという批判もあります。

　『シスター・キャリー』は、18歳のキャリー・ミーバーが大都市シカゴに出てくるところから始まります。車中で知り合ったセールスマンのドルーエと同棲、さらに高級クラブの支配人で家庭のあるハーストウッドとニューヨークに駆け落ちしますが、仕事に失敗したハーストウッドは落ちぶれて自殺、一方キャリーは女優として成功するというストーリーで、このような娘が出世する小説は不道徳だというのが当時の考え方でした。しかしドライサーの書き方にはキャリーを非難したり、ハーストウッドの弱さに同情したりする調子はなく、個人の運命はすべて環境と偶然に左右されるものだとする主張が読みとれます。例えばある晩、ハーストウッドが習慣通りに店の金庫を確認したところ、たまたま鍵がかけられておらず、札束を手にして迷ううちに扉が偶然閉まってしまう場面に、それが典型的に表れています。一方『アメリカの悲劇』の主人公は青年ですが、一人の若者の悲劇を「アメリカの」と題したところにドライサーの意図、つまりアメリカンドリームを追って成功を夢見た若者が挫折し破滅するのはアメリカ社会の悲劇である、と言いたい意図が明確です。

　1951年にウィリアム・ワイラー監督によって映画化された作品（邦題『黄昏』）は、『アメリカの悲劇』の映画版（邦題『陽のあたる場所』）とともに話題になりました。

Theodore Dreiser

(1) 冒頭部分、キャリーがシカゴに向かうところです。

  When Caroline Meeber boarded the afternoon train for Chicago her total outfit consisted of a small trunk, which was checked in the baggage car, a cheap imitation alligator-skin satchel holding some minor details of the toilet, a small lunch in a paper box and a yellow leather snap purse, containing her ticket, a scrap of paper with her sister's address in Van Buren Street, and four dollars in money. It was in August, 1889. She was eighteen years of age, bright, timid, and full of the illusions of ignorance and youth. Whatever touch of regret at parting characterized her thoughts it was certainly not for advantages now being given up. →

Notes ●●●●

1 **Caroline Meeber**「キャロライン・ミーバー」主人公のフルネームです。
  for Chicago「シカゴ行きの」キャリーは列車で数時間の小さな町から、一人でシカゴに向かうことになっています。
3 **baggage car** 客車に連結される「手荷物車」
4 **toilet**（古風）「化粧品、身支度」
5 **snap purse**「（パチンと閉まる）財布」
6 **Van Buren Street**「ヴァン・ビューレン通り」シカゴの中心部を抜けて東西に走る道路の一つ。結婚した姉の住所はシカゴの西側の、軽工業と労働階級や下層中産階級の住宅やアパートの多い地区にあって、夫は精肉工場に通っています。
8– **Whatever touch ... thoughts**「別離に際してのいかなる後悔の念が彼女の考えを特徴づけたにせよ」が直訳です。これでも意味は一応分かります。
9– **it was certainly ... given up**「その後悔は、利益がいま断念されることに対しての後悔ではなかった」

Sister Carrie

→ A gush of tears at her mother's farewell kiss, a touch in the throat when the cars clacked by the flour mill where her father worked by the day, a pathetic sigh as the familiar green environs of the village passed in review, and the threads which bound her so lightly to girlhood and home were irretrievably broken.

To be sure she was not conscious of any of this. Any change, however great, might be remedied. There was always the next station where one might descend and return. There was the great city, bound more closely by these very trains which came up daily. Columbia City was not so very far away, even once she was in Chicago. What pray is a few hours—a hundred miles? She could go back. And then her sister was there. She looked at the little slip bearing the latter's address and wondered. She gazed at the green landscape now passing in swift review until her swifter thoughts replaced its impression with vague conjectures of what Chicago might be. (Ch. 1, p. 3)

Notes ●●●●

11　**a touch in the throat**「胸がいっぱいの感動」a lump in the throat と同じ。
12　**flour mill**「製粉工場」
　　by the day「日決めで、一日いくらで」
13　**passed in review**「視界から消えた」
13– **and the threads ... broken**「そしてついに、糸がきっぱりと切れた」構文としては、tears, touch, sigh と三つ名詞を並べてから、キャリーの心に浮かんだことを順々に挙げてから、最後に「糸が切れた」という一文を置いています。
16– **Any change ... her sister was there.**　ここは全部描出話法です。最初だけ訳せば「変化は、どれほど大きい変化でも、修正できるでしょうよ。どこか、次の駅で降りて戻ればいいのだもの」となります。［英文法ガイド 10-III］参照。
20　**Columbia City**「コロンビア・シティ」キャリーの暮らしていた町の名前です。
21　**What pray is a few hours?**「ねえ、数時間が何だっていうの、何でもないじゃない」修辞疑問です。pray は副詞的に「ちょっと聞くけど」という感じ。［英文法ガイド 10-II-2-C］参照。
24– **her swifter ... might be**「もっとすばやい考えが、車窓に過ぎ行く景色の印象を、シカゴについての憶測で置き換えた」

Theodore Dreiser

(2) キャリーがどんな娘か、作者による説明です。

 Caroline, or "Sister Carrie" as she had been half affectionately termed by the family, was possessed of a mind rudimentary in its power of observation and analysis. Self-interest with her was high, but not strong. It was nevertheless her guiding characteristic. Warm with the fancies of youth, pretty with the insipid prettiness of the formative period, possessed of a figure which tended toward eventual shapeliness and an eye alight with certain native intelligence, she was a fair example of the middle American class—two generations removed from the emigrant. Books were beyond her interest—knowledge a sealed book. →

Notes ●●●●●

1 **Sister** カトリックの修道女を呼ぶときにつけるのが普通ですが、ここでは家族内での愛称として使われていると説明されています。
2 **rudimentary**「未発達の」
3 **Self-interest with her ... strong**「彼女の場合、利己心は高級だったが、強くはなかった」
4 **her guiding characteristic**「彼女の考えや行動を導く特徴」characteristic は名詞です。
4– **Warm with the fancies of youth**「若者特有の幻想で熱くなっている」
10 **knowledge a sealed book**　knowledge の後に省略されている be 動詞を補って読みます。sealed とは、「未知の、不可解な」という意味。
 intuitive graces「直観的に行う優雅なふるまい」

→ In the intuitive graces she was still crude. She could scarcely toss her head gracefully. Her hands were almost ineffectual for the same reason. The feet, though small, were set flatly. And yet she was interested in her charms, quick to understand the keener pleasures of life, ambitious to gain in material things. A half-equipped little knight she was, venturing to reconnoitre the mysterious city and dreaming wild dreams of some vague, far-off supremacy which should make it prey and subject, the proper penitent, grovelling at a woman's slipper. (Ch. 1, p. 4)

Notes ●●●●

11– **Her hands were almost ineffectual**「手を優雅に動かして自分を上品に見せることなど下手だった」ということ。

12– **The feet ... flatly**「足は小さく裏が平らだった」Cf. flat foot「偏平足」

14　**gain in material things**「物質的なものを入手する」

14– **A half-equipped little knight she was**「まだ十分に準備の整っていない、幼い騎士」ここで knight という語を使い、そのイメージでこのあと、reconnoiter（軍隊用語「偵察する」）、prey（「餌食、犠牲者」）、subject（「従者」）などの語を使っていることに注意しましょう。キャリーはこれから、いわば騎士のように戦いに乗り出すのですね。シカゴを征服しようという野望を秘めています。

15– **the mysterious city**（キャリーが好奇心を感じる）「謎の都市」つまりシカゴのことです。

16– **some vague, far-off supremacy**「漠然とした、はるかかなたの支配、覇権」

17　**make it prey ... slipper**「シカゴを、犠牲者、従者、女の足元にひれ伏すまっとうな悔悟者などにする」つまり、魅力的な女が、自分の魅力に降参した男を支配するというイメージです。it はシカゴ市を指します。penitent は、女の魅力に降参し、進んでその言いなりになろうとする男を意味します。

9.『グレート・ギャツビー』

The Great Gatsby
(1925)
by
F. Scott Fitzgerald

　F. スコット・フィッツジェラルド F. Scott Fitzgerald (1896–1940) は、ミネソタ州セント・ポールの名家に生まれました。プリンストン大学に入学しますが、アメリカが第一次世界大戦に参戦した 1917 年、大学 3 年で軍隊に入り、アラバマ州駐屯中に出会った女性ゼルダと婚約、第一作の『楽園のこちら側』(1920) の成功後に結婚します。二人はジャズエイジそのもののような華やかな生活を送りますが、やがてゼルダの精神障害、自身の飲酒癖などが続くうちに借金がかさみ、名声は下降、心臓発作で若くして死去しました。自伝的な傾向の強い作品が多く、後期の傑作『夜はやさし』もそのような一冊です。「失われた世代」の代表で、短編にも優れたものがあります。

　フィッツジェラルドの創作力は 20 年代が絶頂で、派手な生活を支えるためもあって次々と作品を発表しますが、一番の傑作はパリに生活の拠点を移している間に書いた『グレート・ギャツビー』です。中西部の貧しい農家の息子ギャツビーは一代で大富豪となり、自分の出征中に金持ちのトムと結婚していた、かつての恋人デイジーに再び愛を求めるもかなわず、思わぬ死を遂げます。その顛末を、ギャツビーの隣人でやはり中西部出身の青年ニックが語る物語です。ニックはギャツビーと親しくなって共感を覚え、友情をはぐくむようになりますが、冷静な観察者でもあり続けるので、デイジーを美化する一方のギャツビーの目には見えない、デイジーの浅薄な面が読者にも伝わるのです。語り手ニックの存在がこの小説を素晴らしいものにしたと言えましょう。色彩を巧みに使う表現、引き締まった文体も見事ですし、アメリカ東部と中西部の対比も読むことができます。ここに引用したのは有名な冒頭の部分と、ニックが過去というものについてギャツビーと語り合う一節、そして小説の最後の部分です。一度読んだら忘れられない、フィッツジェラルドの洗練された文章を楽しんでください。

　1974 年版の映画『華麗なるギャツビー』は美しい画面が魅力的で、原作の表現もたびたび出てきます。144 分の長い作品ですが、観客を飽きさせません。

The Great Gatsby

(1) 小説冒頭の有名な一節です。

In my younger and more vulnerable years my father gave me some advice that I've been turning over in my mind ever since.

'Whenever you feel like criticizing anyone,' he told me, 'just remember that all the people in this world haven't had the advantages that you've had.'

He didn't say any more, but we've always been unusually communicative in a reserved way, and I understood that he meant a great deal more than that. In consequence, I'm inclined to reserve all judgments, a habit that has opened up many curious natures to me and also made me the victim of not a few veteran bores.

(Ch. 1, p. 7)

*N*otes ●●●●

1 **vulnerable**「傷つきやすい」。前の younger と並んで比較級なのは、どちらも「現在より」の意を含むからです。
2 **turning over**「(心の中で) 考えめぐらす、熟考する」
3 **feel like criticizing**「批判したいような気持になる」
4 **all the people ... you've had**　部分否定です。Cf. All that glitters is not gold.「光るものすべてが金とは限らない」
　 advantages「利点、優位」主に物質的な豊かさ、恵まれた環境のこと。
6– **communicative in a reserved way**「控え目なやり方で意思が通じ合う」
8– **reserve all judgements**「あらゆる批判を遠慮する」
9 **a habit**　前の文の内容と同格です。
　 opened up ... to me「奇妙な人物を僕に近づけた」
10 **veteran bores**　bore は「退屈な人、うんざりさせる人」のことです。veteran は「経験を積んだ、老練な、歴戦の」という形容詞。

F. Scott Fitzgerald

(2) ギャツビーの邸宅でのパーティー後、ニックはギャツビーと二人で話をします。

He broke off and began to walk up and down a desolate path of fruit rinds and discarded favours and crushed flowers.

'I wouldn't ask too much of her,' I ventured. 'You can't repeat the past.'

'Can't repeat the past?' he cried incredulously. 'Why of course you can!'

He looked around him wildly, as if the past were lurking here in the shadow of his house, just out of reach of his hand.

'I'm going to fix everything just the way it was before,' he said, nodding determinedly. 'She'll see.'

He talked a lot about the past, and I gathered that he wanted to recover something, some idea of himself perhaps, that had gone into loving Daisy. His life had been confused and disordered since then, but if he could once return to a certain starting place and go over it all slowly, he could find out what that thing was ...

(Ch. 6, p. 117)

Notes ●●●●

1　**He**　ギャツビーを指します。／ **up and down**　「行ったり来たり」
1-　**a desolate path of ... flowers**　パーティー後なので散らかっているのです。
2　**discarded favours**　「捨てられた記念品」パーティーで配られる記念の品です。
3　**I wouldn't ask too much of her**　wouldn't に「(僕だったら)」の意味を含んでいます。[英文法ガイド 9-IV-3] 参照。
　　ventured　「思いきって言った」反対がありそうなときにあえて意見を言うという感じです。実際ギャツビーは、すぐに反対していますね。
5　**Why**　「なぜ」ではありません。疑問詞ではなく、感嘆詞、間投詞で、ここでは抗議の気持ちをこめて「何だって」くらいですが、他にもいろいろの感情をこめて発せられます。
11　**gathered**　「～であると推測した」
12-　**had gone into loving Daisy**　「デイジーを恋する気持ちになった(理由)」デイジーは、ギャツビーの昔の恋人で、今はトム・ブキャナンの妻です。
13-　**His life had been ... was**　描出話法です。最初の部分は「あれ以来、僕の人生は混乱し、乱れてしまったが、もしある出発点に戻り…」などのように訳せます。[英文法ガイド 10-III] 参照。

The Great Gatsby

(3) 小説の最後、印象的な一節です。

And as I sat there brooding on the old, unknown world, I thought of Gatsby's wonder when he first picked out the green light at the end of Daisy's dock. He had come a long way to this blue lawn, and his dream must have seemed so close that he could hardly fail to grasp it. He did not know that it was already behind him, somewhere back in that vast obscurity beyond the city, where the dark fields of the republic rolled on under the night.

Gatsby believed in the green light, the orgastic future that year by year recedes before us. It eluded us then, but that's no matter— to-morrow we will run faster, stretch out our arms further . . . And one fine morning—

So we beat on, boats against the current, borne back ceaselessly into the past. (Ch. 9, p. 188)

*N*otes ●●●●

- 2 **picked out** いろいろな意味があります。ここでは「識別した」
  green light 対岸にあるブキャナン邸の船着場の先端に輝く灯り。一人芝生に立ってこれをじっと見つめる隣人ギャツビーの姿を、ニックは物語のはじめの方で目撃しています。
- 3– **blue lawn** 月光を浴びたギャツビー邸の芝生を青で表現。この作品で「青」は幸福、理想を連想させる色として使われている、と述べた研究者もいます。
- 7 **the republic** 「アメリカ合衆国」
- 8 **orgastic future** 「うっとりするような未来」orgastic = exciting.
- 12 **So we beat on** 「だから人は、絶え間なく過去に連れ戻されつつも、前進し、流れに逆らってボートを漕ぐのだ」

10.『武器よさらば』

A Farewell to Arms
(1929)
by
Ernest Hemingway

　アーネスト・ヘミングウェイ Ernest Hemingway (1899–1961) はシカゴ郊外に生まれました。釣りや狩猟を好む父の影響で戸外での活動に親しむ一方、音楽好きな母の勧めでチェロを習ったりもしています。高校卒業後、新聞記者となり、1918年には志願してイタリア軍の赤十字に入ります。帰国後にはカナダでの記者時代を経て、特派員としてパリへ行って創作に励みます。最初の短編集『われらの時代に』は最初パリで出版されました。ヘミングウェイの文体はハードボイルドと呼ばれ、主観的感情をおさえて簡潔な点に特色があります。『日はまた昇る』(1926) で有名作家になりましたが , この本はエピグラフ（題辞）に「失われた世代」という言葉が使われていることでも知られています。自身の体験をもとにした小説『武器よさらば』を書いた後には国際政治や社会に目を向けるようになり、『誰がために鐘は鳴る』や、サファリ旅行から生まれた短編などが生まれています。第二次世界大戦後は『老人と海』(1952) でピューリッツア賞を、さらに1954年にはノーベル文学賞を受賞しました。けれども心身の衰えで入退院を繰り返し、1961年に猟銃で自殺して世界を驚かせました。アウトドアを好む男性的なライフスタイルで知られる作家も、内には傷つきやすい精神を持っていたのでしょう。二十世紀のアメリカ文学を代表する文学者として日本でも親しまれています。

　『武器よさらば』は、反戦小説であると同時に恋愛小説でもあります。ヘミングウェイ自身が『ロミオとジュリエット』の現代版だと語っています。建築を勉強していたアメリカ人フレデリック・ヘンリーが、イタリア軍に志願して前線で負傷、イギリス人看護婦のキャサリン・バークレイと真剣に愛し合うようになります。フレデリックは軍を脱走してキャサリンとともにボートでスイスに逃げ、束の間の幸せな時を過ごしますが、難産でキャサリンも子供も失うのです。映画化された作品のうち1957年版は、迫力ある戦場場面と、それとは対照的な美しい風景を背景に、印象的な一編に仕上がっています。

A Farewell to Arms

(1) 小説の冒頭です。

 In the late summer of that year we lived in a house in a village that looked across the river and the plain to the mountains. In the bed of the river there were pebbles and boulders, dry and white in the sun, and the water was clear and swiftly moving and blue in the channels. Troops went by the house and down the road and the dust they raised powdered the leaves of the trees. The trunks of the trees too were dusty and the leaves fell early that year and we saw the troops marching along the road and the dust rising and leaves, stirred by the breeze, falling and the soldiers marching and afterwards the road bare and white except for the leaves. →

Notes •••••

1 **that year** 1917年のこと。主人公で語り手でもあるフレデリック・ヘンリーの回想です。イタリア北部の情景が淡々と描かれていながら、この先を予感させるものが秘められている一節です。
2 **looked across … mountains**「川と平野を隔てて山々と向かい合っていた」
2- **the bed of the river**「河原」
3 **pebbles and boulders**「(水の作用で丸くなった) 小石や丸石」
5 **channels**「河原で水が残って流れている何本かの川」
 Troops went … the road「部隊が家の側を通り、道路を下って行った」
6 **powdered** powderは粉を振りかけることで、ここでは「土ぼこりをかけた」のです。
10 **bare**「何もない」

Ernest Hemingway

→ The plain was rich with crops; there were many orchards of fruit trees and beyond the plain the mountains were brown and bare. There was fighting in the mountains and at night we could see the flashes from the artillery. In the dark it was like summer lightning, but the nights were cool and there was not the feeling of a storm coming.

Sometimes in the dark we heard the troops marching under the window and guns going past pulled by motor-tractors. There was much traffic at night and many mules on the roads with boxes of ammunition on each side of their pack-saddles and grey motor-trucks that carried men, and other trucks with loads covered with canvas that moved slower in the traffic. There were big guns too that passed in the day drawn by tractors, the long barrels of the guns covered with green branches and green leafy branches and vines laid over the tractors. (Ch. 1, p. 7)

Notes ●●●●

15– **the nights ... coming**　夏の稲光なら、暑くてストームが襲うのが普通なのに、ということ。
18　**guns**　トラクターで移動させるのですから「大砲」ですね。
20　**pack-saddles**「荷鞍」

A Farewell to Arms

(2) 前線で怪我をしたため手術を受けたフレデリックと、看護するキャサリンとの会話です。

'We won't fight.'

'We mustn't. Because there's only us two and in the world there's all the rest of them. If anything comes between us we're gone and then they have us.'

'They won't get us,' I said. 'Because you're too brave. Nothing ever happens to the brave.'

'They die of course.'

'But only once.'

'I don't know. Who said that?'

'The coward dies a thousand deaths, the brave but one?'

'Of course. Who said it?'

'I don't know.' →

Notes ●●●●

1　**We won't fight**　「君と僕は喧嘩なんかしないよね」愛し合っていながら喧嘩をする例もある、とこの直前で言ったキャサリンに対しての、フレデリックの言葉。
5　**They won't get us**　「奴らはぼく達を負かせないさ」
7　**They die of course**　「勇気ある人だって死ぬわ、もちろんよ」
8　**But only once**　「でも一回だけだよ」
9　**I don't know**　ここは「さあ、そうかしらね」という意味で、「知らない」ではありません。
10　**The coward dies ... but one?**　「臆病者は千回死ぬが、勇者は一回のみ、のこと？」
11　**Of course. Who said it?**　これは誰が言ったか不明ですが、類似の表現 Cowards die many times before their deaths なら、シェイクスピアの『ジュリアス・シーザー』にあるセリフです。
12　**I don't know**　これは「僕は知らないな」です。

107

Ernest Hemingway

→ 'He was probably a coward,' she said. 'He knew a great deal about cowards but nothing about the brave. The brave dies perhaps two thousand deaths if he's intelligent. He simply doesn't mention them.'

 'I don't know. It's hard to see inside the head of the brave.'
 'Yes. That's how they keep that way.'
 'You're an authority.'
 'You're right, darling. That was deserved.'
 'You're brave.'
 'No,' she said. 'But I would like to be.'
 'I'm not,' I said, 'I know where I stand. I've been out long enough to know. I'm like a ball-player that bats two hundred and thirty and knows he's no better.'

 'What is a ball-player that bats two hundred and thirty? It's awfully impressive.'

 'It's not. It means a mediocre hitter in baseball.'

(Ch. 21, pp. 110–11)

Notes ●●●●

13 **He was probably a coward** 彼とは、この諺を言った人を指しています。
15– **He simply doesn't mention them**「勇者はただそれを言わないだけよ」them = two thousand deaths.
18 **Yes. That's how they keep that way**「そうね。言わないことで勇気を保っているのよ」
19 **You're an authority**「君はこのことでは権威者だな」
20 **That was deserved**「私はその褒め言葉に値したわね」
23– **I've been ... know**「長いこと戦場にいるからわかるんだ」
24 **ball-player**「(プロ) 野球選手」
24– **bats two hundred and thirty**「打率が2割3分」cf. He is now batting .300. ならば three hundred と読みます。.325 ならば略して three twenty-five と読んだりもします。
25 **he's no better**「自分はその程度である」
27 **awfully impressive** 野球に詳しくないキャサリンは、数の大きさの印象で「とっても立派」と言ったのでしょう。
28 **mediocre**「平凡な、並みの」しばしば軽蔑的に「幾分劣った、二流の」のニュアンスがこめられます。

11. 『風と共に去りぬ』

Gone with the Wind
(1936)
by
Margaret Mitchell

　マーガレット・ミッチェル Margaret Mitchell (1900–49) はジョージア州アトランタに生まれました。父は法律家で歴史学者でもあり、南部の伝統的な雰囲気に加えて家族がみな歴史に興味を持つ家庭環境が、後に『風と共に去りぬ』という長大な歴史小説を書くに至る出発点になったことと思われます。スミス・カレッジに入学しますが、母の死をきっかけに帰郷し、『アトランタ・ジャーナル』紙の記者を数年間勤めます。結婚して2年で離婚、1925年に再婚しました。その翌年に足首の怪我で家にいる時間が多くなったのを機会に、調査と執筆に十年以上もかけて完成した作品が『風と共に去りぬ』です。これは激動の時代の精細な描写の中に恋愛の行方も巧みに織り込まれた傑作で、無名作家の初の小説であるにもかかわらず、たちまち全米の、そして世界的大ベスト・セラーになり、1937年にピューリツア賞を受賞、1939年には映画も公開されました。ミッチェルはその後自動車事故で亡くなり、遺された作品はこの一作だけです。

　『風と共に去りぬ』は南北戦争開始の1861年から戦後の再建時代の1873年までの、大きな変動の社会を背景とした恋愛歴史小説で、南部の農園主の長女スカーレット・オハラが主人公です。スカーレットは教養あるアシュレイに憧れていますが、アシュレイが従妹のメラニーと結婚することを知り、メラニーの兄チャールズとの結婚に走ります。が、結婚後間もなくチャールズは戦死、南軍は降伏して、南部は苦しい再建の時代へ。スカーレットはフランク・ケネディと再婚、そしてレット・バトラーと次の再婚へと必死に生き抜くのです。

　原作出版の翌月の映画化権獲得後、3年の歳月をかけて製作された映画は、3時間42分の大作で大ヒットし、今も屈指の名作映画とされています。難航したスカーレット役の女優選び、炎上シーン等の大がかりな撮影など、映画史に残る数々のエピソードがあり、製作費や宣伝費に大金を使うこともこの映画から始まったと言われます。1940年のアカデミー賞で9部門を受賞、またテーマ曲は受賞を逃しはしたものの素晴らしく、映画音楽の古典です。

Margaret Mitchell

(1) 物語の冒頭、南部ジョージアにあるタラ農園のポーチです。

 Scarlett O'Hara was not beautiful, but men seldom realized it when caught by her charm as the Tarleton twins were. In her face were too sharply blended the delicate features of her mother, a Coast aristocrat of French descent, and the heavy ones of her florid Irish father. But it was an arresting face, pointed of chin, square of jaw. Her eyes were pale green without a touch of hazel, starred with bristly black lashes and slightly tilted at the ends. Above them, her thick black brows slanted upward, cutting a startling oblique line in her magnolia-white skin—that skin so prized by Southern women and so carefully guarded with bonnets, veils and mittens against hot Georgia suns. →

Notes •••••

1 **Scarlett O'Hara**「スカーレット・オハラ」この時16歳の主人公。
2 **when caught** = when they were caught.
  the Tarleton twins「タールトン家の双子の兄弟」
2– **In her face were too sharply blended ~**「彼女の顔において、~が鮮明過ぎるくらいに混じりあっていた」つまり、○○は母から、○○は父からというふうにはっきり受け継いでいるということ。倒置文ですね。
3 **features**「容貌、顔立ち」
3– **a Coast aristocrat of French descent** her mother と同格で、「沿岸地域の旧家のフランス人の血を引く人」
4 **ones** = features.
  florid「血色のよい」
5 **arresting**「人目を引く、印象的な」
  pointed of chin「顎がとがっている」of「に関しては」Cf. short of breath「息が切れる」
6 **starred with ~**「~で飾られていた」
8 **cutting a startling oblique line**「驚くような斜線をつけた」そういう印象なのでしょう。想像できますか?
9 **magnolia**「マグノリア」モクレン科の木で、その白い花はルイジアナ州およびミシシッピ州の州花です。
  so prized「とても大切にされて」
11 **Georgia**「ジョージア」アメリカ南部の州名。

Gone with the Wind

→ Seated with Stuart and Brent Tarleton in the cool shade of the porch of Tara, her father's plantation, that bright April afternoon of 1861, she made a pretty picture. Her new green flowered-muslin dress spread its twelve yards of billowing material over her hoops and exactly matched the flat-heeled green morocco slippers her father had recently brought her from Atlanta. The dress set off to perfection the seventeen-inch waist, the smallest in three counties, and the tightly fitting basque showed breasts well matured for her sixteen years. But for all the modesty of her spreading skirts, the demureness of hair netted smoothly into a chignon and the quietness of small white hands folded in her lap, her true self was poorly concealed. The green eyes in the carefully sweet face were turbulent, willful, lusty with life, distinctly at variance with her decorous demeanor. Her manners had been imposed upon her by her mother's gentle admonitions and the sterner discipline of her mammy; her eyes were her own. (Macmillan, Ch. 1, p. 3)

Notes ●●●●

12 **Stuart and Brent**「スチュアートとブレント」タールトン家の双子の兄弟の名前。
13 **Tara**「タラ」スカーレットの生まれ育った農園の名前。スカーレットの父が自分の農園を持った時、もともとアイルランドに実在する地名からとって名付けたものです。
15 **hoops** 女性のスカートに張りを与えて広げるための「輪骨、張り骨」
17 **Atlanta**「アトランタ」ジョージア州の州都。
17– **set off to perfection**「完璧に引き立たせた」
19 **basque**「(バスク地方の衣装を真似た) 身体にぴったりした女性用の上着、胴着」
20 **But for all** ここは but for と続くのでなく、but で切れます。for all が一まとめで「にもかかわらず」の意味になります。
21 **chignon**「シニョン」(仏) 後頭部で束ねる女性の髪形の髷。
23 **carefully sweet face**「注意して優しくした顔」
24 **turbulent**「動揺した、荒れ狂った」
26 **sterner** 乳母のしつけは、母より厳しかったのですね。
27 **mammy**「乳母、ばあや」南部の白人家庭で子守りをする黒人女性です。

Margaret Mitchell

(2) 物語の結びの有名な一節。アシュレイもレットも失ったスカーレットはタラ農園に帰ることに決めます。

 She felt vaguely comforted, strengthened by the picture, and some of her hurt and frantic regret was pushed from the top of her mind. She stood for a moment remembering small things, the avenue of dark cedars leading to Tara, the banks of cape jessamine bushes, vivid green against the white walls, the fluttering white curtains. And Mammy would be there. Suddenly she wanted Mammy desperately, as she had wanted her when she was a little girl, wanted the broad bosom on which to lay her head, the gnarled black hand on her hair. Mammy, the last link with the old days.

 With the spirit of her people who would not know defeat, even when it stared them in the face, she raised her chin. She could get Rhett back. She knew she could. There had never been a man she couldn't get, once she set her mind upon him.

 "I'll think of it all tomorrow, at Tara. I can stand it then. Tomorrow, I'll think of some way to get him back. After all, tomorrow is another day." (Ch. 63, p. 1037)

Notes ●●●●

2– **was pushed ... her mind**「心の上部から除かれた」
4 **cedars**「シーダー」ヒマラヤスギ。
 cape jessamine「ヤエクチナシ」
5 **fluttering** flutter は「ひらひらする、揺れる」
7 **desperately**（口語的）「ひどく」
8– **the gnarled hand on her hair**「乳母の節くれだった手で髪を撫でて（ほしい）」
10– **even when it stared them in the face**「それ（敗北）が顔をまともににらみつけてきても」
11– **She could get Rhett back.** この文を含む3つの文は描出話法です。「レットを取り戻せるわ。できるってわかっている。得ようと私が本気で思いさえすれば、得られなかった男はこれまで一人もいなかったのだもの」[英文法ガイド 10-III] 参照。
13 **set her mind upon** ~ は「~を得ようと本気で思う、心に決める」

12. 『怒りの葡萄(ぶどう)』

The Grapes of Wrath
(1939)
by
John Steinbeck

　ジョン・スタインベック John Steinbeck (1902–68) は、カリフォルニア州サリーナス生まれです。スタンフォード大学では海洋生物学を学ぶかたわら、聖書や古代中世英語にも関心を持ち、当時から詩や短編を書いていました。大学を中退してニューヨークに出ますが出版のチャンスには恵まれず、故郷に戻って再出発、故郷のカリフォルニアを舞台とする『トティーヤ・フラット』(1935) で注目され始め、『二十日鼠と人間』(1937)、『エデンの東』(1952) などが良く知られています。スタインベックには共産主義や社会問題への関心があり、代表作『怒りの葡萄』も資本主義社会における労働者の苦難を描く一編ですが、単なる社会小説ではありません。土に生きる農民を共感を持って生き生きと描き、象徴や寓意もとりいれた作品で、主人公一家に焦点をあてた物語章と当時の社会的背景や移住農民一般を描く中間章とを交互に配置する構成が成功しています。出版されるとたちまち反響を呼んでベストセラーになりました。スタインベックはバラエティに富む題材を、様々の手法で扱うことのできる作家で、1962年にノーベル賞を受賞しました。その後記者としてヴェトナム戦争に従軍、帰国後に死去しました。
　『怒りの葡萄』の主人公のジョード一家はオクラホマの農民ですが、砂嵐とトラクターに追われるように故郷を後にし、一家で夢のカリフォルニアをめざすことになります。元説教師のケイシーを加えた家族全員、全財産を積んだトラックで国道66号線を西へと走りますが、長旅の途中で老人二人を亡くし、何とかカリフォルニアにたどりつくものの、そこでもひどい搾取という苦難が待っているのです。
　ここに引用したのは、淡々とした大地の描写がまるで印象派の絵画のような冒頭の一節、及び一家がようやくカリフォルニアの地を踏んだ場面です。
　ジョン・フォード監督による映画化は、配役、演出も見事で、アカデミー最優秀監督賞、最優秀助演女優賞（マー・ジョード役）を獲得するなど、各方面で激賞されました。

John Steinbeck

(1) 冒頭の一節。乾いた大地の描写に色彩を効果的に使っています。

  To the red country and part of the gray country of Oklahoma, the last rains came gently, and they did not cut the scarred earth. The plows crossed and recrossed the rivulet marks. The last rains lifted the corn quickly and scattered weed colonies and grass along the sides of the roads so that the gray country and the dark red country 5 began to disappear under a green cover. In the last part of May the sky grew pale and the clouds that had hung in high puffs for so long in the spring were dissipated. The sun flared down on the growing corn day after day until a line of brown spread along the edge of each green bayonet. The clouds appeared, and went away, and in a 10 while they did not try any more. The weeds grew darker green to protect themselves, and they did not spread any more. The surface of the earth crusted, a thin hard crust, and as the sky became pale, so the earth became pale, pink in the red country and white in the gray country. (Ch.1, p. 1) 15

*N*otes ●●●●

1 **the red ... the gray country**「赤の地帯全部と灰色の地帯の一部」
  Oklahoma「オクラホマ」アメリカ中南部の州。ジョード一家の故郷です。しかし、長い干ばつが一帯を襲い、多くの農民たちがこの地を離れなくてはならないことになります。
2 **cut the scarred earth**「干からびた地面を切りこむ」ここでの cut は、雨が地面にしみ込んでいくこと。
2– **the plows crossed ... marks**「細い川のあった痕跡の上を鋤(すき)が行ったり来たりした」乾いた地面の上に僅かな雨が降った後の様子です。
3– **lifted the corns**「トウモロコシを芽吹かせた」
4 **scattered weed colonies and grass**「雑草の群れと牧草をばらまいた」
6– **the sky grew pale**「空の色が薄くなった」
7 **had hung ... long**「ふわふわした大きな塊になって長い間浮かんでいた」
9 **a line of brown spread**「茶色の線が(葉の縁に沿って)蔓延した」
10 **bayonet**「銃剣」ですが、ここでは銃剣のように先のとがったトウモロコシの葉。
11 **they did not ... more**「現われては消えるという動きを、それ以上は止めてしまった」

(2) ジョード一家がカリフォルニアの地を初めて目にする場面です。

 Al pulled to the side of the road and parked.
 "I want ta look at her." The grain fields golden in the morning, and the willow lines, the eucalyptus trees in rows.
 Pa sighed, "I never knowed they was anything like her." The peach trees and the walnut groves, and the dark green patches of oranges. And red roofs among the trees, and barns—rich barns. Al got out and stretched his legs.
 He called, "Ma—come look. We're there!"
 Ruthie and Winfield scrambled down from the car, and then they stood, silent and awestruck, embarrassed before the great valley.

*N*otes ●●●●●

1 **Al**「アル」ジョード家の三男で16歳。トラックの運転ができます。
  pulled to ... road「道の端に（車を）寄せた」
2 **ta** = to.
  her 土地を女性にたとえて she を用いることがあります。
2– **The grain fields ... in rows** 眼前に広がる景色の中に見えるものを列挙しています。
3 **willow lines**「柳の並木」
4 **Pa** = Dad, Daddy.「父さん」一家の当主で働き者の父親です。
  knowed = knew. 訛りです。
  they was anything like her「それらがこんな風だとは（知らなかった）」they が指すのは、前述の grain fields などや、後述の peach trees などでしょう。漠然とした表現です。
6 **rich barns**「（納屋といっても）立派な納屋」
8 **Ma** = Mom, Mama.「母さん」ジョード一家の中心。
  We're there「（目的地に）着いたよ」
9 **Ruthie**「ルーシー」12歳の次女。
  Winfield「ウィンフィールド」末っ子で10歳の少年。
10 **embarrassed**「どぎまぎして」立っているときの様子。付帯状況を表わす過去分詞構文です。［英文法ガイド 5–I–4］参照。

John Steinbeck

→ The distance was thinned with haze, and the land grew softer and softer in the distance. A windmill flashed in the sun, and its turning blades were like a little heliograph, far away. Ruthie and Winfield looked at it, and Ruthie whispered, "It's California."

Winfield moved his lips silently over the syllables. "There's fruit," he said aloud.

Casy and Uncle John, Connie and Rose of Sharon climbed down. And they stood silently. Rose of Sharon had started to brush her hair back, when she caught sight of the valley and her hand dropped slowly to her side.

Tom said, "Where's Ma? I want Ma to see it. Look, Ma! Come here, Ma." Ma was climbing slowly, stiffly, down the back board. Tom looked at her. "My God, Ma, you sick?" Her face was stiff and putty-like, and her eyes seemed to have sunk deep into her head, and the rims were red with weariness. Her feet touched the ground and she braced herself by holding the truck-side. (Ch. 18, pp 250–51)

Notes ●●●●

11 **The distance was thinned with haze**「靄で距離が減らされた」つまり遠方のものが近くに見えたのです。
13 **heliograph**「日光反射信号機」
15 **moved his lips ... syllables**「口の中で数語をつぶやいた」
17 **Casy**「ケイシー」元説教師。一家と共に旅をしてきました。
  Uncle John「ジョンおじ」50歳。妻を失い、一家と共にやってきました。
  Connie and Rose of Sharon「ローズ・オブ・シャロン」本名は「ローザシャーン」ですが、こうも呼ばれています。ジョード家の長女でコニーの妻。身籠っています。
  climbed down「はい降りた」登る時なら climb up、降りる時は climb down です。climb を上り下り両方に使えるのですね。
21 **Tom**「トム」ジョード家の次男。殺人罪で仮出所してきて物語に登場します。
22 **back board**「(トラックの) 後板」
23 **My God**「これは、これは!」驚きを表わす間投詞。
24 **putty-like**「(窓ガラスの固定に使う) パテのよう」
25 **rims**「目の周り、縁」
26 **braced herself**「身体を支えた」

英文法ガイド

1 5つの文型 ……………………………………118
2 動詞（完了形）………………………………119
3 不定詞 ………………………………………120
4 分詞（現在分詞・過去分詞）………………121
5 分詞構文 ……………………………………122
6 動名詞 ………………………………………124
7 受身 …………………………………………125
8 関係代名詞・関係副詞 ……………………126
9 仮定法 ………………………………………128
10 時制の一致・話法 …………………………130
11 代名詞 ………………………………………132
12 コンテクスト ………………………………132

1 5つの文型

Ⅰ 第1文型 (S＋V)　主語＋完全自動詞

1. I swim in the swimming pool.「私はプールで泳ぐ」in the swimming pool は修飾語句。
2. The baby cries often.「赤ん坊はよく泣く」

Ⅱ 第2文型 (S＋V＋C)　主語＋不完全自動詞＋補語

1. She is a doctor.「彼女は医者だ」
2. Tom looks happy.「トムは幸せそうに見える」
3. My son will become a teacher.「息子は教師になるでしょう」

Ⅲ 第3文型 (S＋V＋O)　主語＋完全他動詞＋目的語

1. I eat an apple a day.「私は1日に1個リンゴを食べる」
2. Jane always answers my e-mail.「ジェインはいつも私のメールに返事をくれます」
3. Tom changed trains at Tokyo Station.「トムは東京駅で乗り換えた」

Ⅳ 第4文型 (S＋V＋O＋O)
　主語＋完全他動詞＋間接目的語＋直接目的語

1. I gave him a pen.「私は彼にペンを与えた」
   直接目的語が先にくると、I gave a pen to him. となる。give の他 bring, show, teach, tell, write などは to となる。
2. He buys her a doll.「彼は彼女に人形を買ってあげる」
   直接目的語が先にくると、He buys a doll for her. となる。buy の他 cook, find, get, make などは for となる。

Ⅴ 第5文型 (S＋V＋O＋C)
　主語＋不完全他動詞＋目的語＋補語。

1. Everybody calls her Betty.「みな彼女をベティと呼ぶ」
2. She keeps her room clean.「彼女は部屋をきれいにしている」
3. The news made her happy.「その知らせは彼女をハッピーにした」

2　動　詞（完了形）

I　現在完了　have, has ＋ 過去分詞

1. I *have* just *finished* lunch.「ちょうどランチを終ったところだ」
2. She *has lost* her passport.「彼女はパスポートをなくしてしまった」
3. *Have* you ever *seen* a lion?「きみはライオンを見たことある？」
4. I *have known* her since she was a child.「ぼくは、彼女が子供の時からずっと知っています」

例文 1. は完了、2. は結果、3. は経験、4. は継続を示す。1. と 2. は似ているが、2. は「パスポートを無くして、今もとっても困っている」という紛失の結果をも問題にしている。

II　現在完了進行形　have ＋ been ＋ 現在分詞

She *has been studying* since morning.「朝からずっと勉強している」
これは She *has studied* since morning. も継続用法なので同じ意味だが、「まだ勉強している」というニュアンスの継続の事実を強調している。

III　過去完了　had ＋ 過去分詞

1. The train *had* already *started* when I arrived at the station.「わたしが駅に着いた時、列車はすでに出発していた」（完了）
2. She found that she *had lost* her passport.「彼女はパスポートを失ってしまったのを知った」（結果）
3. I *had* once *seen* a lion before that occasion.「その時より前に、一度ライオンを見たことがあった」（経験）
4. She *had studied* English for four years when she went to New York.「彼女がニューヨークに行った時、（それまで）4年間英語を勉強していたのだ」（継続）

3 不定詞

I to 不定詞の用法　to + 動詞の原形

1 名詞的用法

主語　*To eat* this cake or not,that's the question.「このケーキを食うか食わぬか、それが問題だ」

補語　My dream is *to see* Miss Elmer again.「ぼくの夢は再びエルマー先生に会うことだ」

目的語　She wanted *to study* abroad.「外国で学ぶことを望んだ」

2 形容詞的用法

I want *something to drink*.「何か飲むものが欲しい」

3 副詞的用法

目的　I *got up* early *to catch* the train.「列車をつかまえるために早く起きた」

原因・理由　She was *happy to see* me.「わたしに会って彼女は大喜びだった」

結果　My mother *lived to be* 86 years old.「母は86才まで生きた」

4 be + 不定詞　命令、可能、予定など。

You are to go.「行け」「行ける」「行く予定だ」

II to なし不定詞（原形不定詞）

1 知覚動詞 + 目的語 + 原形不定詞

I *saw her walk* away.「私は彼女が歩き去るのを見た」

2 使役動詞 + 目的語 + 原形不定詞

I cannot *make him change* his mind.「彼の気を変えさせられない」

III 不定詞の実質上の主語を示す for

It is necessary for Mary to go now.「メアリが今行くことが必要だ」

4 分　詞（現在分詞・過去分詞）

I 形と種類

現在分詞　動詞の原形＋ ing（動名詞と同じ）。
過去分詞　規則的—動詞の原型＋ ed（過去形と同じ）。
　　　　　不規則的— break → broken, begin → begun など。

II 分詞の用法

1 形容詞用法　名詞の前後にあって形容詞の働きをする。

1. Let *sleeping dogs* lie.「眠っている犬」
2. There are still *broken buildings* in Kobe.「こわれたビル」
3. The *girls playing tennis* are my cousins.「テニスをやっている娘」
4. Tom has a *watch made in Switzerland*.「スイス製の時計」

2 主格補語　come, go, sit などの動詞＋補語。

1. The dog *came running* to me.「犬は私のところに走って来た」
2. She *looked tired*.「彼女は疲れてみえた」

3 目的格補語　知覚動詞（see, hear, feel など）＋目的語＋分詞。

1. We *saw him dancing*.「彼が踊っているのを見た」
2. Did you *hear my name called*?「私の名が呼ばれるのを聞いた？」

4 have, make, get ＋目的語＋分詞

1. I *had my hair cut*.「髪を切ってもらった」
2. Can you *make yourself understood* in English?「英語で人に理解してもらえますか？」

III excite「興奮させる」、surprise「驚かす」など感情を表す他動詞の分詞

1. We are all excited at the news.「知らせに皆興奮している」
2. Tom is an exciting dancer.「トムは（人々を）興奮させる踊り手だ」
3. How surprised we are to hear that Alice has got the prize!「アリスが賞を取ったと聞き、いかに驚いていることか」
4. Snoopy is a surprising dog, because he can speak English.「英語が喋れるので、スヌーピーは驚くべき犬だ」

5 分詞構文

2つの節からなる文を分詞を使って簡単に表現する。理由、時、条件などを表わす。

I 用法

1 理由

Being ill, he did not go out.
= *As he was ill*, he did not go out.「病気なので彼は外出しなかった」
Written in Latin, the book is difficult to read.
= *Since it is written in Latin*, the book is difficult to read.「ラテン語で書かれているため、その本は読むのが難しい」

2 時

Walking in the park, she saw many birds.
= *While she was walking in the park*, she saw many birds.「公園を歩いている時、彼女は多くの鳥を見た」
Surrounded by eager fans, the singer felt very happy.
= *When she was surrounded by eager fans*, the singer felt very happy.「熱心なファンに囲まれた時、歌手はとても幸せに感じた」

3 条件

Turning to the right, you'll find the house.
= *If you turn to the right*, you'll find the house.「右に曲がれば、その家が見つかるでしょう」
Left alone, the little girl will begin crying.
= *If she is left alone*, the little girl will begin crying.「もし一人ぼっちにさせられたら、その子は泣き出すでしょう」

4 付帯状況

We stayed there for some time, *kissing each other*.「私たちはたがいにキスしながら、しばらくそこにいた」
The girl came into the office, *accompanied by her mother*.「その娘は、母親につきそわれて、オフィスに入って来た」

[注意] 時、理由などと一応分類したが、絶対的にそうだというのではないので、前後関係から正しい意味合いを推測するのがよい。

II 2つの節の主語が違う場合（独立分詞構文）

Night coming on, we returned home.= *When night came on*, we returned home.「夜がやって来た時、私たちは帰宅した」

It being rainy, we cannnot go on a picnic.= *As it is rainy*, we cannnot go on a picnic.「雨なのでピクニックに行けない」

III 慣用的表現

Generally speaking, Tokyo is a noisy city.「一般的に言うと東京はやかましい都市だ」

Talking of books, have you read *Kokoro*?「本と言えば、きみ『心』を読んだ？」

6　動名詞

形は現在分詞と同じで動詞の原形 + ing だが、名詞の働きをする。

1 主語

　Walking is good for health.「歩くことは健康によい」

2 目的語

　1. 他動詞の目的語
　　She enjoyed *watching TV*.「彼女はテレビを観ることを楽しんだ」
　2. 前置詞の目的語
　　I am fond of *drinking beer*.「私はビールを飲むことを好む」

3 補語

　My hobby is *collecting coins*.「私の趣味はコインの収集です」

4 名詞の前についた場合

　a *waiting* room「待合室」, a *sleeping* car「寝台車」
　※ただし a sleeping baby は「寝ている赤ん坊」であり、この sleeping は現在分詞である。

5 動名詞を含む慣用表現

　1. on ~ing「～するや否や」「～した時」
　　On hearing the news, we were all shocked.「そのニュースを聞いた時、みんなショックを受けた」
　2. cannot help ~ing「せざるをえない」
　　I *couldn't help laughing* when I saw the funny dog.「その奇妙な犬を見て、笑わざるをえなかった」
　3. There is no ~ing「することが出来ない」
　　There is no smoking here.「ここでは禁煙です」

7 受 身

受身の形　主語＋be＋過去分詞

1 さまざまな時制

1. 現在　The dog *is loved* by Mary.「犬はメアリに愛されている」
2. 過去　The meeting *was held* in Tokyo.「会は東京で開かれた」
3. 現在進行形　My car *is being washed* by the machine.「車は機械で洗われているところだ」
4. 過去進行形　My son *was being examined* at the hospital.「息子は病院で検査中だった」
5. 未来　More people *will be saved* from now on.「これからはもっと多くの人が救われるでしょう」
6. 現在完了　The cake *has* just *been taken* out of the oven.「そのケーキはオーブンから取り出されたばかりだ」
7. 過去完了　I found that I *had been robbed* of my purse in the train.「車中で財布を盗まれたと知った」

2 by 以外の前置詞

He *is known to* everybody. ← Everybody knows him.「彼は有名人だ」
The ground *is covered with* snow. ← Snow covers the ground.「地面が雪に覆われている」
Wine *is made from* grapes.「ワインはぶどうで作る」（材料がすぐ分からない）
The table *is made of* wood.「そのテーブルは木製だ」（材料がすぐ分かる）
We *were surprised at* the news.「その知らせに驚いた」
Nancy *was born in* 1985.「ナンシーは1985年生まれだ」
I *am interested in* animals.「私は動物に興味を持っている」

3 日本語との表現法の違い

My son *was killed* in the war.「私の息子は戦死した」←「殺された」
I *was bored*.「私は退屈した」←「退屈させられた」

8 関係代名詞・関係副詞

I 関係代名詞
1 種類・格

先行詞	主格	所有格	目的格
人	who	whose	who（口語）whom
動物、物	which	whose of which	which
人、動物、物	that	なし	that
なし（先行詞を含む）	what	なし	what

1. Here is *a dog that* was born a week ago. 「ここに一週間前に生まれた犬がいる」
2. I have *an aunt who* is very kind. 「とても親切な叔母が私にはいる」
3. We keep *a dog whose* father won a championship. 「その父が選手権を取った犬を飼っている」
4. That is *a desk (which)* I bought yesterday.「これが私が昨日買った机だ」この which のように、目的格は省略されることが多い。とくに会話体ではきわめて多い。
5. This is *what* I wanted to eat. 「これは、私が食べたかったものだ」

2 that のこと

上の表のように that は先行詞の別なく用いるが、先行詞に最上級、all, only などがある時は、必ず that を用いる。

1. This is *the only money that* I have now. 「これしかお金がない」
2. You are *the most handsome man that* I have met. 「会った中でもっともハンサムな男ですね」

3 前置詞＋関係代名詞

This is the house. He lives in it.
この2つの文を関係代名詞を用いて合わせると、This is *the house in which* he lives. または This is *the house (which)* he lives *in*. となる。

II 関係副詞

1 when（時）

Do you know *the time when* the movie starts.「映画の始まる時間を知ってますか」

2 where（場所）

This is *the place where* I first met the girl.「ここが、その娘に初めて会った所だ」

3 why（理由）

There are *some reasons why* I refuse.「わたしには、断わる理由がいくつかあります」

4 how（方法）

Show me *how* we can open the safe.「どうすれば金庫を開けられるか教えて」

9 仮定法

I 仮定法過去　If ＋ S ＋過去形、S ＋ would など＋原形

現在の事実に反する仮定を表す。

1. *If I were* rich, *I would* give you money.「もし私が金持なら、きみに金を与えるところだ」

    過去形は、be 動詞の場合はどの人称でも were を用いるが、口語では was もよく使われる。ただし If I were you だけは決まり文句になっているので If I was you とは普通言わない。

2. *If she worked* hard, *she would succeed.*「もし懸命に働けば、成功するだろうに」

II 仮定法過去完了　If ＋ S ＋過去完了、S ＋ would など＋ have ＋過去分詞

過去の事実に反する仮定を表す。

1. *If I had been* rich, *I would have helped* you.「もし金持だったら、きみを援助してあげたところだ」

    現実は、金持でなかったので、援助しなかった、という「過去の事実」をふまえている。

2. *If she had worked* hard, *she would have succeeded.*「もし懸命に働いていたならば、成功しただろうに」

    現実には、さぼったために、失敗したという事実をふまえての表現。

III 仮定法でない If

1. *If* it is true, I will apologize to you.「それが本当なら君にあやまる」
2. *If* you know the answer, please tell me.「もし答を知ってるのなら、教えてよ」
3. *If* she said so, she was telling a lie.「もしそう言ったのなら、嘘をついていたのだ」
4. *If* you should fail, let me know.（未来）「万一失敗するようなことがあれば、知らせて」

Ⅳ 仮定法の慣用表現

1 I wish ＋仮定法

I wish I *were* a bird.「鳥ならいいのに」
I wish I *had been* rich.「金持だったらよかったのに」

2 as if ＋仮定法

He speaks English as *if* he *were* an American.「アメリカ人のように英語を話す」
Don't treat me *as if* I *was* a child.「私を子供みたいに扱うのはやめてくれ」

3 if の省略

Were I a bird [= If I were a bird], I *would fly* to you.「もし鳥ならば、私はあなたのところに飛んで行くところだ」
A wise mother *would* have scolded her son then.「賢い母ならその時息子を叱っただろうに」
To hear him talk, you *might* think he is a rich man.「話だけきけば、金持ちだと思うかもね」

4 If it were not for, But for, Without など。

If it were not for air, all animals *would die*.「もし空気がなければ、すべての動物は死ぬであろうに」
Without water, no one *could live*.「水がもしなければ、誰も生きられないだろうに」

5 丁寧、遠慮、曖昧を表す

Could you tell me the way?「道を教えて下さいませんか」Can you tell me the way, please? よりもより丁寧な感じである。
She *might be* his mother.「もしかすると彼女は彼の母なのかもしれない」「彼女は彼の母だとしても不思議はない」

6 祈願文　主として決まった表現に限る

God help the Queen!「神が女王をお助け下さいますように！」

10　時制の一致・話法

I　時制の一致

1　規則通り

He *says* that he *is* ill. → He *said* that he *was* ill.「自分は病気だと彼が言った」

I *think* that he *told* a lie. → I *thought* that he *had told* a lie.「彼が嘘をついたと、私は思った」

2　規則の例外（不変の真理、現在の習慣など）

The teacher *said* that the earth *moves* around the sun.「地球は太陽の周囲を回っているのだと先生が話した」※ moves → moved とならない。
Mary *said* that she *always goes* to bed at 11 : 00.「メアリはいつも 11 時に就寝すると言った」※ goes → went とならない。

II　直接話法→間接話法

1　平叙文

A. 一般的な場合

He says, "I am kind." → He says that *he is* kind.「自分は親切だと、彼は言う」

He said, "I am kind." → He said that *he was* kind.「自分は親切だと、彼は言った」

B. 仮定法の場合

She said, "If I *were* a bird, I would fly to you." → She said that if she *were* a bird she would fly to me.「もし自分が鳥ならば、あなたの所へ飛んで行く、と彼女が言った」
B. は仮定法なので「時制の一致」の規則に従わない。

2　疑問文

A. 疑問詞のある場合

"Who *put* sugar in my tea?" she said. → She asked who *had put* sugar in her tea.「私のティーに誰が砂糖を入れたの、と彼女が言った」

B. 疑問詞のない場合

"*Can* you swim" Tom asked me. → Tom asked me *if / whether* I *could swim*.「トムが、きみは泳げるのと私に訊ねた」

C. 修辞疑問 (Rhetorical Question)

疑問文だが、答は分かっていて、嫌味で尋ねる場合がある。

How can a man of 100 carry such a heavy chair?「100 歳の老人にはこんな重い椅子は運べないのに」

3 命令文・依頼文

A. 命令

"Wash your hands, Tom," she said. → She told Tom to wash his hands.

B. 依頼

"Please introduce yourself," he said to her. → He asked her to introduce herself.「彼女に自己紹介をやって下さい、と彼が言った」

C. not が入っている場合

She said to us, "Don't be noisy." → She told us not to be noisy.「うるさくしてはいけない、と彼女が我々に言った」

Ⅲ 描出話法

物語の中などで、作中人物が思ったり感じたりしたことを、例えば、He said to himself, "Mary is very kind." と直接話法や、He thought that Mary was very kind. と間接話法で述べないで、Mary was very kind. と書くことがある。作者による客観的な描写でなくて作中人物の思いである。これが描出話法で、「メアリはとても親切だな」、「メアリって、本当に親切だわ」などと、話し手の感想として訳すのが普通。

11 代名詞

1 一般の人を指す you

「一般の人」を指す代名詞は、we, they, one もあるが、you が好まれる。You can't make an omelet without breaking eggs.「卵を割らないでオムレツを作れない」この you がその好例。次の場合のように、判然としないこともある。

You must love your parents. 一般論なのか、親不孝な「君」に忠告しているのか、コンテクストによる。

2 あらたまった場合に使う one

One should always do one's best.「人は常に最善を尽くすべきだ」

3 I を使うのが自己主張が強いと思い、やや気取って使う one

What was one to do when all one's friends had lost their money?「友人が皆破産した時、(私に) 何ができただろうか」

4 問題になっていることや、内面にあるものを指す it

電報を見て真っ青になった妻を見て夫が、What is it? と尋ねた場合、it は決して電報を指さず、真っ青になった原因、問題を指す。「それは何だ」でなく、「何なの?」「どうした?」などと訳すべき。

12 コンテクスト (文脈、前後関係)

「蛙の子は」に続く言葉は何か、と問われたら、「蛙」と答えるのが正解なのは、国語の試験というコンテクストの場合であり、もし理科の試験というコンテクストなら「おたまじゃくし」が正解です。

映画化された英米文学 24
そのさわりを読む

編著者　行方 昭夫
　　　　河島 弘美

発行者　山口 隆史

発　行　所　　株式会社 音羽書房鶴見書店
〒113-0033　東京都文京区本郷 3-26-13
TEL 03-3814-0491
FAX 03-3814-9250
URL: https://www.otowatsurumi.com
e-mail: info@otowatsurumi.com

2016 年 3 月 1 日　初版発行
2023 年 4 月 1 日　6 刷発行

©2016 by Akio Namekata & Hiromi Kawashima
組版・装丁　ほんのしろ
印刷・製本　（株）シナノ
■落丁・乱丁本はお取り替えいたします。

F-079

[不許複製]